CHASING

MY ROOKIE YEAR

THE MICHAEL CLAYTON STORY

Library of Congress Cataloging-in-Publication Data
Michael Clayton, Chasing My Rookie Year

Edited by: Candi Clark, Karen R. Thomas, Ashanti Clayton & Taylor Hadnot

Published by: Soul Writers, LLC: PO Box 291835 Tampa, FL 33687

10 9 8 7 6 5 4 3 2 1

Printed in the United States of America

Note: This book is intended only as an informative guide for those wanting to know more about life. Readers are advised to consult a professional life coach or counselor before making any changes in their life. The reader assumes all responsibility for the consequences of any actions taken based on the information presented in this book. The information in this book is based on the author's life experiences. Every attempt has been made to ensure that the information is accurate; however, the author cannot accept liability for any errors that may exist. The facts and theories on life, love, business and success are subject to interpretation, and the conclusions and recommendations presented here may not agree with other interpretations.

CONTENTS

PREFACE

In 2004, I was a first round draft pick out of Louisiana State University. I was 15th overall in a draft ripe with wide receivers such as Larry Fitzgerald, Roy Williams, Reggie Williams, and Lee Evans. The irony is that although I was the 15th to be selected, I played better than any of the other wide receivers in my rookie season. That year I caught 80 passes for the Tampa Bay Buccaneers and was not only named the team MVP, but also the runner-up for NFL Rookie of the Year to Ben Roethlisberger. I led all rookies in receptions, yards, and touchdowns.

But then I began to experience injuries and coaching changes; at that very moment, my career took a different course from what I expected. This book's purpose is not to make excuses, but rather acknowledge responsibility for my own actions and share intimate details about my life and experiences in the National Football League (NFL). The reality is that I never had another season like my rookie season- not even close. Knee injuries, turf toe, and fractured fingers were all a part of my personal journey.

After my rookie season, people constantly asked me, "When are you going to get back to your rookie year?" Throughout my eight-year career as an NFL player, I chased my rookie year with the desire to have another one like it. I wanted to be selected for the Pro Bowl and I wanted to win the Super Bowl. I never made it back to that level of production again. I dropped from 80 to 32 catches my second season and never wowed a crowd again like I did that rookie year. Although I had some good moments, nothing was like the collection of moments during my rookie season.

The NFL taught me many valuable lessons. I never asked for a second chance at an NFL career because football alone never defined me. I was a great human being before the NFL. My NFL experience taught me that greatness goes above and beyond ones' own ability on the gridiron. There are other ways to be a productive team member. I found that mentoring younger players with the Bucs and New York Giants was also vital to the success of the team even if my own personal career was lackluster. I refused to allow my own personal issues to negatively impact my attitude towards my teammates. For me, chasing my rookie year is a metaphor for the quest for greatness I pursued my entire life.

I am still chasing my rookie year and that is fine because I have discovered a purpose that goes above and beyond the game of football and being in the spotlight. Now I strive to be the star that shines after the stadium lights are off. As I reflect on what motivated me, I felt compelled to share my story in the hopes of guiding other athletes to supersede my rookie year.

During my lifetime pursuit of excellence, I learned valuable lessons from my successes and failures. In fact, I learned the most important lessons in life during the failures. It was not only the failures that taught me, but also the mayhem, hardship and tragedy I endured.

I firmly believe that we cannot see around life's every corner so we should prepare for the unknown with good habits, strong work ethic and honesty. Thank you for taking the time to read this book. May God keep you and bless you for I am just a vessel.

ACKNOWLEDGMENTS

First, I would like to say thank you to all the coaches I have ever had throughout my life and career. They have all played an intricate role in my growth as a player and person. Those who have had a lasting impression include Coach Malen (Choo-Choo) Brooks from the South Baton Rouge Rams, coach Greg Ironside, Tony Knox, and David Barham from Christian Life Academy. Thank you to Coach Stan Hixon for believing in me and making me set high standards for myself. You made me a leader in my room at a young age and taught me "G.A.T.A". I would also like to say that the mentality you instilled in me was what I was known for in my 8 years in the NFL. Thank you so much.

To Jimbo Fisher for all of your support throughout my high school years. You have been in my corner and to this day, you have never left my side. Thank you for allowing me to be a part of your success in building your legacy at FSU. To my beloved Coach Richard Mann; if I had to write what you mean to me, I would have needed to write a whole other book. You coached me when I needed to be coached and you fathered me when I needed to be fathered. You befriended me when I needed a friend. What you do goes without merit. Thank you for what you do for the game of football. Coach Rich Basachia (Dallas Cowboys) at the lowest moment in my career, you found a way to motivate me and pick me up through special teams. You gave me purpose again and made me remember why I love the game of football again. Thank you for believing in me.

To John Gruden, thank you for giving me the opportunity to show my talent to the world. I know at times we didn't always agree, but I always appreciated your tough love. It made me a better man and always allowed me to go the extra mile and really create character within myself.

To coach Raheem Morris (Washington Redskins), thank you for the opportunity to continue my journey with the Bucs. My family is truly grateful for that. The two players that pushed me in my life to go above and beyond in my career were Marcus Spears and Corey Webster (NY Giants). I didn't know who I was athletically until I met Marcus Spears. He helped me understand who I was at a young age and set a high standard mentally and athletically. To Corey Webster; I've admired you since we were kids. You always carried yourself as a consummate professional even at a very young age. I want to thank you for the war we used to go through at every practice since our days at LSU. I wouldn't have achieved half my success if it wasn't for your friendship and willingness to work with me. We made each other great. I am proud of the men both you and Marcus have become. As all three of us come from the same walk of life, may this book inspire the both of you to continue to do great things, and inspire others off the field.

It was a pleasure getting to know the New York Giants organization. Thank you for allowing me to be a leader within myself. To Coach Coughlin, thank you for taking the time to get to know me as a person and as a player. You didn't have to take a chance on me, but you did and I am truly grateful for the opportunity to play under your leadership. You have set an unprecedented standard for my life.

I would like to thank Coach Saban. It seems like yesterday, (2001) thirteen years ago when you sat in my living room and told me to make a 40 year decision in coming to LSU and not a 4 year decision in going to Florida State. You told me that the great people of Louisiana would never forget if we met our goal of winning a national championship. That day, you convinced me to follow you, and you led me to success, not only in football but in life. Under your mentorship, I learned how to be a consummate professional- the greatest asset I ever known.

To my parents, Milton and Marjorie Clayton, younger sister Marcie, older brothers Marcus and Snow; without you, none of this would be possible. The love, guidance, support, and lessons I've learned through your strength and belief in God is what got me to where I am today. There is not a day that goes by that I am not thankful to have such wonderful people in my life.

I would like to thank my godmother Mrs. Betty Lodge and the entire Lodge family for the spiritual guidance in my life. Your obedience to God always resulted in a special word for me that has been life changing. I love you guys.

To my In-Laws Tennyson & Gwendolyn Wright, you have set an example of what family is all about. Both of you have stepped in and have gone over and beyond the call of duty as parents and grandparents, giving Tina and I the opportunity to chase our dreams. My children adore you and Tina and I would not know what to do without you.

Lastly, to my wife Tina and our children, Madison, Michaela, and Michael II; you are the reason I wake up smiling every day. I thank you for the love and support you give to me as a husband and father. I will continue to work hard to make sure you will always have everything you ever want in life, and I dedicate this book towards your future of success. May God continue to bless us as a family.

DEDICATION

This book is dedicated to every parent who desires to improve their children's lives. My hope is that the child, who experienced the pain of an absent parent, may begin to see their own true potential for greatness as they look past their parent's flaws. As single parents, I dedicate this book to you in hopes of sharing a few words of inspiration and confirmation that your dedication, sacrifice and perseverance is valued. For the person that is soul searching and trying to make sense of life, I hope that my experiences might be a lens to see your success.

By looking into my life as I chase my rookie year, I hope that someone can learn from my mistakes and accelerate their growth as much as humanly possible. As parents struggle to lay a Christian foundation for their children, I hope that you continue to believe that all things are possible through the love and mercy of Christ.

INTRODUCTION

There is a purpose, and order to life. You have heard it before; "God has a plan for us". That is the essence of Michael Clayton. Now let me go on the record and state that I am a man of faith, following a path that has been cleared for me. I am not the only one holding my life's compass; God is my guidepost. This is why I believe I did not drown at the age of two when I fell into a pool. I could have become just another accidental death- a news flash across the screen: *A Two Year Old Drowns in Neighbor's Pool.* God had plans for me. I do not remember the incident because of how young I was, but I have heard the story over and over. In fact, I have heard it so many times that I feel like I can almost remember that day. The story goes something like this:

It was a Sunday and I was roaming freely in the yard with my older brother, Marcus and his friends. There were not many fences back in those days. Neighbors were neighbors and we did not shut each other off with property lines or barriers. Mom let my brother and me play freely in the yard thinking that we would never leave the yard. As I wandered around the yard, I caught a glimpse of the house behind our back yard. In the neighbor's back yard rested a place of serenity for any kid in Louisiana during the summer time: a swimming pool. Now a swimming pool was rare back in the day for us. The closest we ever got to a swimming pool was the puddle at the end of the Slip n' Slide we made out of dad's old tarp and mom's dish-washing detergent.

As I approached the neighbor's yard, I can only imagine what I was thinking, "It is hot. I gotta feel that water." As I walked up to the pool, I was unknowingly staring at a bloody murderer who had taken so many children's lives. Suddenly, Mrs. Betty darted out of her back door screaming, "Michael, Michael, get away from there!" My godmother ran to me, scooped me into her arms and captured me from death. I wonder if God whispered in Mrs. Betty's ear:

"Betty, look out the window at the boys playing ball. Where is Michael? Now look in the corner of the window. Lean forward so you can see behind the tree that is obscuring your view. There he is! Michael is about to jump in the pool. Go get him. Please!"

I do not know where I would be if Mrs. Betty had been lazy that day or planned to vacuum in another room instead of doing the dishes. I thank God for His perfect order from the time I wake up until the time I close my eyes at night.

I often wonder what my parents' lives would have been like without me - their little one playing ball in the house breaking everything on the shelves; or my older brothers' lives without their little brother; or my precious baby sister, who would have no one to play Barbie with her. Yes, you read correctly. I said Barbie. All of the things I would achieve, all of the things I would bounce back from after failure, all of the people I would love and help...all of it would never have occurred if my next door neighbor had not decided to wash the dishes at that particular moment.

My belief and personal conviction lead me to conclude that things are ordered and happen just the way they do: like a quick thought that causes a person to run back into the house to grab a bag avoiding a tragic accident as he or she might think, "That could have been me!" I am alive because of God's order and plan for me.

Knowing how close I came to death - two feet, two seconds - I value my time on this earth differently than others who have not had near death experiences. I have often wondered, "Why me?" or "Why not me?" and in so many cases I received the answer through triumph and sometimes pain. In this case, I did not understand for many years why I was rescued from death. As I grew older and saw how each of us can impact our friends, families and communities, I came to understand that God had a plan for me. There would be some mystery to it, like that rookie year. But I could recognize and sense a great power. Even as a young kid in Baton Rouge, I sensed that

I was not alone. I believe there was a whisper Mrs. Betty heard that day as I believe there have been whispers to me throughout my life.

This book is about those whispers and trying to make sense of things. These are priceless lessons I learned. From the smallest to the greatest things that occur in our lives, everything that happens to us has a purpose. I also believe that if we can align ourselves to a purpose, we will see the result on our personal journey. Please notice that I said "purpose," not dreams, aspirations, wants or likes. I have learned that in many cases, dreams, aspirations, wants and likes are only stepping stones for us to fulfill our purpose. Purpose is not always pretty; it is a journey full of trial and error. My Christian beliefs taught me that Christ paved the way for me to define my purpose. Because this world can be so challenging and unforgiving at times, I believe that each individual has the ability to control how their story is written. The never-ending question that people should ask themselves is, "How good will my story be?"

THE EARLY YEARS: LEARNING TO MAXIMIZE MY POTENTIAL

Always Go Above and Beyond

When I was 15, I was a cart collector for Sam's Club. Customers would leave them up against curbs or in the far corners of the parking lot. If you have ever shopped at Sam's Club, you know how those metal carts can get left everywhere. Sometimes people would put them in the corral and you just had to tug them out of there, which was no easy task for a 175-pound kid who did not have his man muscle.

I could have slacked and maybe left that cart in the corner of the parking lot for the next guy, but I did not. I had an excellent work ethic. Maybe that is one of the reasons I made it to the big time NFL. I wanted to be better than the next guy. I did not cut corners like a lot of kids my age; instead, I stepped up the level of work I did.

I made sure the cart area was full of carts at all times, even if that meant pushing in 50 carts at a time. It was not just a job to me; it was a proving ground. I loved competition, even if I was just competing against myself.

Although my primary duty was cart collector, I also hustled inside and helped cashiers bag customers' groceries. Then, I helped the customers put their groceries into their cars, and I was mindful not to just throw the groceries into the car any kind of way; I stacked them nice and neat, making sure nothing would spill or break. The thing that made my actions stand out so much was Sam's Club did not even offer this service. I was just motivated to be the best cart guy the store ever had.

Never once did I accept a tip out of a customer's hand because it was store policy that we could not accept tips. Notice I said I never accepted money out of a customer's hand. When a customer offered a tip, I would explain that we could not accept tips. You discover a lot about people when you are honest with them. Some customers would get in their car, say "Thank you" and drive off. Most customers would stuff money into my pocket and say, "Well, it is not a tip; it is a gift." Other customers would throw money on the ground and say, "Young man, you dropped something." There is not much you can do except pick up the money. But, heck, I would have given them 100 percent effort without the tips.

I served customers with a smile and positive attitude. It got to the point that people would come in and request me by name. How about that? Some things make you proud of yourself. How many children today are missing that lesson? They are waiting for somebody else to say, "I am proud of you." Well, why not do a good deed and say it in the mirror, "I am proud of you." Customers wanted me to be their bagman and push their cart to their car. I took pride in that, and it paid off. Throughout my life, I would realize that when you do more than what is expected, great things happen.

My favorite people to see at work every day were Mr. Al and my manager Mr. Remy. Mr. Al was sixty plus years old and wore a green wave Tulane hat every day. He used to tell me, "Tulane would love to give you a scholarship!" I just smiled, and said, "Alright Mr. Al." when I was really thinking, "Yeah right Mr. Al". Mr. Remy would make sure we had Gatorade in the cooler instead of water for those hot summer days. The irony in all of this is, my first game in college was against Tulane. When I came down the legendary "tiger walk" before the game, there stood Mr. Remy and Mr. Al, working as volunteers for the LSU staff greeting us as we entered the locker room doors. They were there working as greeters for every home game throughout my college career. I would hear through the grapevine how they both would rave about me to the LSU staff about my work ethic from working with them at Sam's. I did not understand it then but I do now; my fate was set and my reputation preceded me. People were investing in my future and speaking positive things into existence, before I could say, "Hello, my name is Mike." The staff accepted me from day one with open arms and welcomed me into the LSU family. Maybe this is why I made it to the big show, being a joy to others just as much as they have been a joy to me.

I was not so good when I first started playing organized football so I practiced everyday on my own until I became one of the best. I still can hear my dad saying, "Sports are not for everyone. If it were that easy, everyone would do it, so if you want it, pay the price." Hard work and a good work ethic allowed me to live out my dream of playing football.

In school, I knew people expected me to be a simple-minded jock. Ok, I was not the brightest apple on the tree, but strived to be the sweetest apple. I can honestly say that I was far from the highest achieving student. My mom would say, "No girl in her right mind wants a knuckle-headed young man." My high school English teacher Mrs. Devitt would reiterate my mom's word throughout high school career to make sure I did not forget it. I was determined to improve my academics even if it meant reading things four to five times before I understood it, and that is exactly what I did. In fact, I even asked my classmates to teach me their good study habits because I wanted to defy the stereotype people had of athletes. With all of this effort, I made Honor Roll in high school and The Dean's List at LSU. With this level of determination and persistence, I was eligible to accept my football scholarship; however, in order to keep that scholarship and achieve my dream of going to a prestigious college, I had to keep the momentum moving forward. The truth is I worked really hard and I refused to be labeled as just another dumb jock.

Here is the other stereotype I wanted to defy: the athlete as a selfish "punk". So I worked at trying to treat people with respect and kindness to the utmost and many times I succeeded. It is how I wanted to be treated. It is a state of mind, really. The rewards are abundant, a favor upon my life. Through sound friendships, relationships and mentorships, I have been able to create my foundation, Generation Next, which serves youth in Baton Rouge, Louisiana, New York, New York and Tampa, Florida.

When one decides to go above and beyond the minimum level, high achievement is possible. I found that as I went above and beyond the minimum standard, my commitment was constantly tested with temptation, setbacks and insults. It can be tough to make sound decisions when you have worked hard and roadblocks keep popping up. Trust me, I have been there. My resilience has been tested throughout my life. The reality is that I lost some battles and I won some. There was a constant duel within myself - "Am I doing the right thing?" I often failed, but I realized that falling is not failure as long as I got back up!

I have found that it is very common in life to do just enough to get by. We do just enough to edge out the person next to us. We can make a habit of it. In school, we may only shoot to pass classes instead of getting all A's. In practice, we may only try to be faster than the slowest girl or guy. At work, we may do only what is asked or required of us. But I remember hearing this quote, "Shoot for the moon, and if you miss, you will still be amongst the stars." That was me, I was blessed that way. I believe that we should compete against ourselves and against a higher standard, not the minimum requirement. When running a 40 yard sprint and everyone else starts to fall behind at 30 yards, do not think the race is won; push even harder.

Do not be afraid to be great. One should always strive to raise the bar by going the extra mile. I started doing that with carts at Sam's and soon going above and beyond became a habit. I realized that if I did extra the first time, I thought it was hard; the second time around, it was not so hard; and third the time, it became part of me – a habit. I once heard that there is no traffic on the extra mile and found it to be true while in college when I was named All-Southeastern Conference, which is pretty respectable if you ask me. Not many people are willing to go above and beyond to beat the competition, so take pride in going above and beyond. Look where it can get you: All-SEC. Third-team All-American, First-round draft pick. I did all those things by running, not walking, along the extra mile.

Take pride in being the best student one can be. Take pride in being the best son/daughter one can be. Take pride in being the best athlete one can be. That is what the world needs most: more people to take pride in their lives and go above and beyond. Remember this: pride has nothing to do with skill, and nothing to do with being able to run a 4.4-second 40-yard dash or out-jump a defensive back for a ball. Pride is detached from skill. Pride is satisfaction something has been achieved that others admire.

It takes a conscious effort to become an NFL player, and unfortunately plenty of players with talent fizzle out before they get to the NFL. Look at all the players in the league who were not drafted, but yet made it onto rosters over all the players that were drafted. They made a conscious effort to do more.

What I realized over the years is that practice makes habit, not perfection. Whatever you do repeatedly will become who you are, so practice the way you want to perform, not only in sports, but also in life. If you live your life in a mediocre way, you will be mediocre. Strive to be extraordinary, and you will at least catch excellence. Remember, what got you here won't keep you here. You always have to do more. If you settle, you just might get stuck! It is worth the effort to try and get better every day.

We have all heard of a "bust," or someone who is not performing at the level of his or her preconceived expectation. At one point, people labeled me a "bust" because they judged me only for my "on the field" production. My rookie season, I caught those 80 balls and that was the expectation for me the rest of my career. Now this is where I am going to defend myself because I want to put the simple facts on the table. I had 11 different quarterbacks in my six years with the Tampa Bay Buccaneers, two of which were the starting quarterback twice. We suffered a lot of injuries and we had coaching changes and new schemes. The truth is that at times, things beyond my control dictated my future. What fans did not see is that I brought other qualities to organizations, so teams kept me around. The proof I can offer that I was not a "bust" or a "cancer" to the Tampa Bay organization is that the Bucs gave me a new deal even with my numbers falling off. What most people did not know is that I was taking young players under my wing and helping them grow as professionals. In my eyes, this ultimately made our team closer, stronger and more competitive. Even without gaining thousands of yards and making 200 more catches in my career, I was still rewarded with new contracts. I got a roster spot on a Super Bowl winning team because of my contributions off the field and trying to do things beyond what I was hired to do. My work ethic got me to the NFL and kept me there for years.

HARD WORK BEATS TALENT

You've probably seen the movie *Rudy*. Rudy was the smallest guy on the team, but he had a big dream. Everyone doubted him, even his closest family members. Yet, Rudy did not care about what they had to say because he just wanted to play. He went to practice early and left late. Rudy lifted extra, ran harder and went all out every day. In fact, he worked so hard that he earned the respect of his teammates. They were not going to play if he did not get to play. Rudy's hard work motivated everyone around him; he was a leader even though he was not the best player on the team. Rudy's story proved that hard work beats talent. So imagine if you are talented at something and work hard at it. The sky is not even the limit.

I can relate to Rudy. I know, it doesn't sound possible. People remember me as one of the best athletes in Baton Rouge, the state of Louisiana, and a high school All-American who was recruited by every major university. Before I grew several inches, though, I was a sorry little athlete. My family would go over to Mississippi for family reunions and the kids would play football from sun up to sun down. Those cousins of mine rocked me. They hit hard and they meant business. I was not accustomed to such hard hitting and being thrust into that type of competitive environment, I can honestly say that I was not the best player on the team.

As I began to play organized sports, I was not the most athletic guy on the team, but I learned to outwork everyone around me. It started when I was 9 years old playing Pop Warner Little League Football with the South Baton Rouge Rams. Everyone on the Pop Warner team was from a rough neighborhood, had a "mean dog" mentality, and was naturally gritty. They were a scrappy bunch of kids. Then, there was me. I grew up in a neighborhood with no chaos or crime, just a bunch of neighborhood kids trying to find the biggest yard to serve as our all-day Sunday football field. We were a little bit soft compared to kids from other parts of Baton Rouge.

Thanks to my dad's foresight to buy one of the largest houses in the neighborhood with one of the biggest yards, our yard was home field advantage every Sunday. Fortunately, my brother Marcus and I knew where to run to hit the slight slopes and where if you hit it just right, it felt like you hit the B button (*Speed Burst Button*) on Sega. We also knew where the holes were that would pretty much tackle you if you ran through them.

However, I quickly learned that playing organized football was much different from playing in my back yard with no pads, no coach and no real rules. I will never forget the day my dad dropped me off in South Baton Rouge where the Pee Wee Rams held their practice.

I cried as his black Chevy Blazer drove off up the hill. He left me with this man named Maleene Brooks better known as Coach Choo. He was not just strict; he was the meanest, toughest but best Pop Warner coach around. Although he did not play around with us, words cannot explain what this man did for me and what he means to me. He worked with a lot of players who would later do big things in college and the NFL. Warrick Dunn, the All-American with Florida State, the All-Pro with the Bucs and Falcons, was one of many other standout players that he worked with.

From the moment I stepped on the field, Coach Choo called me Chiney-ball chest, a name I despised even though I was a skinny little kid. Soon I decided that I had to be just as mean, if not meaner, than the other kids. I had to out-work those guys to make it on that field and make a new name for myself. Maybe this is where I learned to do extra.

It was a scorching day; the whistle blew and everyone gathered around since it was time for the hitting drill. Guys lined up across from each other and ran full speed into one another like rams butting heads. Just my luck Coach Choo said, "Give me Chiney-ball chest and Big Derrick Perkins." Now Derrick was the starting linebacker who hit so hard he could have played with the 13-and-older group. We were only 9. My stomach dropped; I was scared, but there was nowhere to run and backing down now would make me the laughing stock of the team. Besides, who wants the name "scary little Chiney-ball chest?"

I heard "Hut!" and I sprinted forward, closed my eyes and gave Big Derrick Perkins all I had. When I came to, we both stood there with crazy looks on our faces. He looked surprised because he had never lost or tied a hitting drill. My look was one of astonishment, too; I was still alive. Everyone went wild even Coach Choo. He probably was expecting me to be laid out on the ground. He was excited, and he smiled and yelled "Ooooohh!

Then he yelled, "Again! Again!" This time, big Derrick and I hit so hard that you could hear it echo, and we both flew back. Everyone started screaming in amazement. Before I knew it, I was one of the hardest hitters on the team, and good ole Coach Choo never put Big Derrick and me against each other again for fear of someone getting seriously hurt.

After this drill, I started to pride myself on my hitting. I went from "Chiney-ball chest" to a "sleazy-yellow-dawg" as Coach Choo put it. I had found that dog in me. I was not the fastest; I was not the strongest; I was not the biggest; I just faced down my fears. I worked like success was not mine and I had to take it even if the odds were stacked against me. I learned at an early age that hard work beats talent any day. You can ask anyone who ever played the game with or against me, on any level, how I played from that point on. I played the game of football from that day with vengeance, forcing my will upon my opponent. Imagine that, little ole Michael Clayton became a junk-yard dog on the gridiron!

REMAIN HUMBLE IN ALL YOU DO

I also learned my first lesson in humility playing Pop Warner. Coach Choo, also known as Attila the Hun, the one who demanded I hit and play hard did not tolerate the Hollywood style on his football team.

I was getting good on the football field and was full of confidence. I used to watch the college guys do their thing on the field at Alcorn State University. They would play so emotionally and after making a big play, they would showboat after a big run or catch and pound their chest like cavemen after a big hit. They were writing little sayings, scriptures and reminders on their gloves, shoes and, sometimes, bodies. I loved it because it made the game feel so much more authentic. So, I decided to express that same emotion when I played. That was a bad idea in front of Coach Choo.

One game I had a huge hit on a guy. I came across him and just laid into him. I hit him with everything I had. You could hear the echo from the field. It felt good; I felt powerful. I felt like I was playing for my favorite team, Alcorn State University. I thought I was the man, so I showed it by showboating and doing my thing. I wanted to soak up that moment and get some extra attention for that amazing hit I had just laid on that dude.

Coach Choo did not let me have my moment. He called me to the sideline, grabbed my face-mask, took a mouth full of chewed up catfish he was enjoying on the sideline and threw it into my helmet. He proceeded to shake my face-mask until the fish just oozed down my face. He yelled at me and said, "What's wrong with you?

You ain't never hit nobody before? Cut that mess out and play ball!" I was shocked; I thought he would be yelling in amazement like he did in the hitting drill with Big Derrick Perkins. I had it all wrong; he was more professional than that. He showed respect to our opponents no matter how badly we beat them. Seconds after he threw the fish he removed my helmet, wiped my face with his shirt in a loving and fatherly way and apologized for getting so riled up.

Now I recognize that some may say the coach's behavior was unacceptable and I am not condoning this type of reaction, but this one experience that had a significant impact on me for the rest of my life. That day, Coach Choo taught me to always remain humble no matter how good I got. From that day forward, I would slap my chest and point to the sky after a big play to tell God, "Thank you!"

To me, humility is keeping a respectful attitude about yourself and others. Too often, athletes are arrogant and self-absorbed. Because so many stereotypes exist about professional athletes, people do not expect athletes to greet people and open doors or stop to sign autographs. I like it when I surprise people with some genuine respect. It comes from being humble and grateful. I believe we should embrace and respect those around us as well as the environment. People should not feel beneath athletes simply because a person may have less money, success or status.

As a Christian, I believe what the bible says concerning humility. Proverbs 15:33 reads, "Humility comes before honor." What that means to me is that honor and glory come only when a person is humble. Humility will take you places that talent cannot. Coach Choo helped me understand humility. I believe that a large part of my success, on and off the field, is due to my humility. I got chances and opportunities in football, sometimes when it looked like others deserved it, mainly because I had a humble attitude about life.

Sadly, many athletes do not embrace this character trait. Have you ever seen an athlete who has all of the talent in the world, but as soon as something bad happens, he is dropped like a hot potato and never picked back up because no one liked his attitude? I can think of a few, but I won't name them. I am sure you can think of the same ones I am thinking of. These guys seem to expect a red carpet to be rolled out for them everywhere they go, even on the practice field. They are rude, mean, condescending, self-centered, and selfish.

There are athletes who are really good at what they do and make a lot of money. Then, one day the individual gets injured or begins to get old overnight and cannot get a break because they are not good for the team's morale; they are only valuable because of their athletic skills. It is sad to see, but it happens all the time. Then it is payback time. The people they took advantage of have no time for them and eventually tell them, "Hit the road, Jack."

On the other hand, look at a guy like NBA player Grant Hill who I believe is humble. He appears to be nice and mild-mannered. Grant comes in, does his job and goes home. Grant seldom gets called for technical fouls. I do not see Grant in the media making bogus claims or getting in trouble. Grant Hill has had injuries and missed games, yet he has kept his job. He was paid to sit on the sideline hurt for so many games and seasons. How does this happen for some and not others? I believe that it is his attitude. Attitude means more than anything else. The attitudes of people like Grant Hill are prime examples of how humility comes before honor!

My dad constantly told me, "Act like you have been there before!" He was referring to the end zone and glory. He was letting me know that those who are prepared and have worked hard on their craft expect to succeed and do not go all silly with theatrics when they make a play. So to actually succeed should not be such a surprise that you behave inappropriately.

In college, often the big man on campus is known for getting all the girls and looking down on the nerds, but I was taught to be the exact opposite. I was nice to the kids others called nerds. I befriended them, and we studied together and we supported each other. I was definitely not a bully. Instead, I protected the kids being bullied. Often, I would get their lunch money back or give them some of my food. It is just how I was raised. Because I found real strength within myself, I did not feel the need to make anyone else around me feel inferior. Instead, I wanted to make them feel strong just like me.

Humility is the essence of my upbringing. My dad worked for the United States Department of Agriculture and my mom was an educator. They had good jobs and could afford to buy me things, but we would get hand-me-down clothes from my cousins. When those bags of clothes came to the house, we were excited. We learned to appreciate small things and be thankful. Other kids had the name brand clothes, but it did not matter to us.

My parents instilled in me a spirit of gratitude and sharing.

My dad often became a caretaker for some of my friends who did not have a father in their house. He shared his time and whatever we had with kids who had so little. Kids relied on him so much they called him "Pops." Once he taught my best friend Ike how to catch fly balls and Ike turned out to be a pretty good baseball player.

I realized that there is real strength in humility. When we are strong enough in our glorious moments to show class and respect for others, that is when we are really powerful. Showboating, bragging, and looking down on others is a weakness, not a strength. Arrogance is a weakness and will ruin your life if you do not get it under control quickly and turn it into confidence.

So, I encourage you to be humble in all you do. Treat everyone how you want to be treated. If you do not treat yourself good, treat the other person the way they want to be treated. Do not walk with your chest poked out and a frown on your face. Instead smile, laugh, play, and have fun with the people around you. Be nice to people for no reason at all and enjoy how you throw them off guard. Listen to your coaches, bosses and teachers. Learn how to change a bad habit and show people you are listening. This will take you further than you can ever imagine! Doors will be opened for you!

One of the great wastes of time is the college football player who does not take advantage of the future business contacts he can make in college. They go to class, well, most of the time they go to class, and then they go to practice. Players do not always take advantage of the opportunity to learn from other people. Because I decided to be humble and open to the people I met along the way in my career, I can do business today with many people from all walks of life. I can earn money and live a good life.

As I think back, I remember a lot of football players who were guarded, rude, and looked down on people because of their status as an NFL player. I decided to be different so I carried myself differently, and it is paying off now when I really need it to.

What is the percentage of NFL players who go broke three years after they are out football? Over 70 percent go broke and that is so sad. From my perspective, it was the choices they made.

As you live your life, know that the way you treat others will eventually come back to you. It can be good or bad for you. The good news is that it is your choice regarding what you will receive based upon what you give. Keep that in mind as you live your life and are building your future. Remain humble in all you do!

COLLEGIATE YEARS: WITH EVERY LOSS, THERE IS A GAIN

Losing My Loved Ones

L ife requires sudden courage. We all want to live happily ever after, but then there are these interruptions, terrible interruptions. They happen quickly, without warning and we better learn to cope, and have some inner heroism. You know what I am talking about. You have this narrative in place...friends *walking up the mountain with you, life being a breeze* and then, just like that, you are blind-sided - someone dies. I do not believe that a person is ever as unsettled in life as the moment a close loved one dies.

This chapter is about my loved ones who have been called to God. I am holding the memories close of Marquis Hill, Steve Williams, Dave Peterson, big bro Kevin Weeks and my grandparents: Big Papa, Big Mama, and Mama

Geneva. I am holding onto the lessons I learned with Marquis and Steve's sudden deaths. I am holding tight to the memories of the spirit and resolve my grandparents displayed in old age.

We all handle death differently. Some are able to only focus on the positive memories of the ones they've lost; others go into depression. Some never recover. To date, I have lost five friends. I want to share a few stories that taught me significant and bitter lessons that had a profound impact on me. As of today, I have recovered... I think.

I was recruited by Louisiana State University (LSU) and signed with my hometown school. I became one of the best ambassadors for the football program because I could persuade high school athletes that LSU could not only be a national powerhouse, but a terrific place to spend four years of college. I was living a dream and nobody knew better than me. I was having fun and we were winning games. The Tigers would win a national title in 2003 and I was in the middle of it as a wide receiver. I was the only receiver in LSU history to have 700 yards receiving in three straight seasons. It was high times for me and I shared this joy with LSU recruits, especially the defensive tackle Marquis Hill. I recruited him hard for the Tigers and he signed. I felt a sense of responsibility for Marquis, right up until the day he died.

I became really good friends with two guys: Ben Wilkerson (center) from Hemphill, Texas and Marquis, who was from New Orleans. Marcus Spears (tight end/

defensive lineman) from Baton Rouge was already a close friend and the four of us were inseparable.

Ben and Marcus were already convinced that they needed to come to LSU, but Marquis was still undecided. He was a big-time player, a 6-foot-5 pass rushing marauder and Coach Saban and the staff really wanted him. I say Marquis was not sure if he wanted to go to LSU, but maybe he was just acting like he was undecided just to see how badly LSU really wanted him. Some kids do that; it is part of the process.

We needed him to complete our signing class and he was holding out on making his official commitment. I felt sure I had already convinced him to come to LSU, but he wanted to see the coaches sweat the day he made an unofficial visit. "Mike watch this," he said. Marquis turned playful. He yelled to our offensive coordinator, Jimbo Fisher, (now head coach of Florida State), "Man I ain't coming here. Jimbo, you tryin' to switch me to tight end, aint'cha?" I watched Jimbo's face turn red. He did not know what to say back to this prized recruit. He really liked Marquis and wanted him badly to wear the purple and gold, and there was Marquis just playing with old Jimbo. I just shook my head and laughed. We had Marquis.

Marquis would later sign his scholarship with the Tigers and all four of us, Marcus Spears, Ben Wilkerson, Marquis Hill and I, became roommates at East Campus Apartments (ECA), "the legendary Room 604". We would all play in the NFL. Marquis was the life of the room. Not a day went by without us falling on the floor laughing until we cried. Marquis was one of the funniest guys I have ever met. We lived in that apartment two years. We both were taken in the 2004 draft. He was a second round pick of the Patriots and I went in the first round to Tampa Bay.

So now I am at the part of the story where I needed some of that sudden courage I mentioned at the start of this chapter. It was May, 2007, after my third year in the NFL, and my friend Steve Williams called me at my house in Tampa. I was in the kitchen. "They cannot find Marquis," Steve said. Marquis had gone jet skiing in Lake Pontchartrain with a friend, Ashley. They were late coming home. No one could find them.

Finally, in the middle of the night, rescuers found Ashley clinging to a buoy in the lake. She and Marquis had fallen off the Jet Ski in the early evening, just after dark. They were not wearing life jackets. Ashley told rescuers that Marquis had pulled her toward a buoy and told her to hold on. She did not remember much, except that she suddenly couldn't hear Marquis. They found his body the next day. The doctors said he had a nasty bruise above his eye and that he probably suffered a concussion, which negated his powerful ability as a swimmer. It was ruled an accidental drowning; my college roommate was dead at the age of 23.

It is a bitter memory for me because once we got to the NFL, Marquis and I did not talk as much as we used to. My life happened; his life happened. I took things for granted because I thought I would connect with 'Quis' one of these days. He was north with the New England

Patriots and I was south with the Tampa Bay Buccaneers. We thought we would have time to relive some of our LSU escapades. It is one of my lasting regrets that I let our friendship fade. It hurt me even more to know that he had left a son behind and I did not know that son. I was one of Marquis' closest pals.

To this day, I feel my stomach drop when I get a late night call. Some unfamiliar number will flash across the face of my phone and I think, "Do I really want to take this call?" Unfortunately, Steve's call about Marquis was not the last phone call I would dread. I would need more courage. My grandparents were next: my dad's mom, then my mother's mom and dad. Their deaths hurt me to the core because of how devoted they were to their grandchildren.

My grandfather, who we called Big Papa, was a preacher at Rose Bower Church. To my family it was known as Rose-uh-ba. During Big Papa's Sunday morning sermons, he said, "UummmNaaaaaaa" after every other word. He always had a smile on his face. I would kiss him on the forehead every time I would go out there on the weekend to see them in McComb, Mississippi because I had so much respect for him. My mom was a daddy's girl and I could see why. Sometimes we would go on Friday and stay through the weekend. I just remember the long service on Sunday and his sermons were always very passionate.

I will never forget the time that he pulled me aside to have what would end up being a "Come to Jesus" moment. He called me aside and said, "Seven, come in here". He called me seven because I would have my big momma make me seven peanut butter and jelly sandwiches before my hour and a half drive back to Louisiana. It was weird that my grandfather pulled me aside because we never really had a man-to-man talk before. He said that he had a few quick things that God had put on his heart to tell me, and I was all ears.

I was so excited to hear the news because I thought that he was going to tell me I was going to be a famous football player or superstar – man was I wrong. He asked me if I remembered Dr. Quinn's family, the one that my grandmother worked for. My grandfather looked at me and said very seriously, "Not only is it the family that your grandmother worked for, but your mother and all my daughters. Not to mention that we have this land he let me buy off him that you boys have been running up and down all your lives. That old white man was one of the most decent men I have ever met, gave me a lot to be proud of here in Mississippi, and I was proud to call him my friend."

He went on to explain the only difference in people is decent and indecent; he told me to never pay the indecent any attention. He said the Lord told him that there was a young lady that I was fond of and to not be uncomfortable because she was a different color. As he said this, my heart dropped. How did he know about her? How did he know what I was going through? This issue was something that I would only think about in private and never express to others.

As our man-to-man conversation came to an end, he said something that will stay with me forever, "Do not ever be afraid of who you are. You're a decent young man and just the way God intended you to be." My whole body got the chills. I could not understand how he knew about something so small, but so impactful. I began to cry. For God to care about me so much to send the message in the form of my grandfather had me overcome with joy. At that moment, my grandfather helped me to understand that I was highly favored – a realization that has brought me peace in my darkest hours. I feel like he had a feeling that I was going through a tough time.

Big Papa also taught me about tithing and helping people. I was burdened to think that the only way to help others was with money. This conflicted with my ability to provide for myself, so I became confused. He told me, "Listen, it is time and talent, not just money." He released this burden on me. I knew to give time and talent, not just money. He brought me peace.

Then, there was his wife, Big Mama, who was known for her biscuits. She would make about 100 of Big Mama's Saturday and Sunday morning biscuits. You were sorry if you slept in, so sorry you cried, because if you slept in, the biscuits you waited for all week for were gone. She was a soft, gentle, courageous woman. My mother and all of my aunts took on my grandmother's character traits. Guess that's why all of their homes felt like home to me growing up and still do to this day.

Then, there was Mama Geneva and her $25 and $50 Christmas cards that she never missed sending. We received those cards until the year she died and God called her home. The memories of these loved ones, these fine people, helped ease my pain when it was their time to go.

I was hurting, but I could look back with fond memories. You know I was afraid of my cousins at one time. We would visit and when it was time to go to sleep I would walk down a dark gravel road to my grandparent's house just to stay with them. It hurt me to tears watching them grow old and watching them not be able to go outside and see the sunshine.

I felt differently with each of these experiences. In my grandparents' case, it hurt to see what they had to endure: the pain; the long days of their bones aching from lying in a hospital bed; the embarrassment of not being strong enough to get up and go to the bathroom; the helplessness of relying on their children and eventually hired help to care for them; the loneliness of being in their bedroom all day with only a window to see daylight. It killed me inside to see them not able to live their lives as they used to, so I was a bit content they no longer had to suffer.

In my roommates' case, I felt the need to tell my friends I loved them every time we talked, not knowing whose tomorrow would not be promised. Throughout my career, I would receive more of these devastating phone calls. It taught me not to take people for granted.

I would like to tell you about one more call that changed my life forever. Steve "The Prince" Williams got his nickname from his father who was somewhat of a "King" in the tough streets of South Baton Rouge, also known as "The Bottom." No one went to The Bottom unless they lived in The Bottom. It could be a pretty raw and uncut place.

I met Steve through my best friend, Ike, when I was around 10 years old. Steve became really close to Ike, which allowed our friendship to grow. We would soon call ourselves brothers. I did not really know what Steve was doing when I went to LSU. He was just around. He was not enrolled at school while I was there, but it was like he attended LSU as many times as I saw him on campus. The Prince might not have been a football player, but he was still part of the team, part of the group. He helped the football players with schoolwork and went beyond just being a friend. He was like a brother not just to me, but also to a lot of them.

When I was drafted in 2004 (15th overall), I hired my friend Courtney Trask to help me out with the details of signing the contract with Tampa Bay. I felt Steve was my responsibility because he met everyone at LSU through me. So I brought him with me to Tampa. I could not leave him behind. You just do not take anybody. Steve came with me because he was so smart. I paid for him to go to real estate school. Then I met my wife and my homeboys left. There were a lot of friends that wanted to go with me, but he was the one who was most responsible.

Steve was one of the smartest dudes I ever met. He was valedictorian of his high school and knew about everything in the world. That was crazy to me because of his background, you know coming up in The Bottom. I was proud of him. Steve impressed me with his own smarts, but being around his dad gave Steve a lot of street knowledge, sometimes more than he could handle. Steve was going to play a big part in my next business venture. I felt he needed a little boost to enter the lifestyle of the rich and famous. He had the know- how.

I wanted my closest friends to experience everything I had. My cars were their cars, and my house was their house. Their clothes were my clothes, mostly because I worked and never had time to shop. Steve and Courtney would say, "I just cannot understand why a millionaire steals clothes from a man with five dollars in his pocket." If it was in the closet I would pop the tag and put it on. They were kidding, of course. This was my way of showing them I needed them. In my heart, I always felt like I was doing the right thing for my friend Courtney would pay all my bills and make sure the house was taken care of. So why did I feel so empty? Why was I drinking? Was I not giving enough money to people and spreading my God-given fortune? Was I an alcoholic? All I thought I was doing was a little weekend binge drinking. It was a time for me to drown my problems away. I did not have to worry about the pressure and the media. Things were bad with the Bucs after that first season and I was missing success. I was not achieving goals and the alcohol on the weekends was my answer to my newfound reality.

Some weekend nights, Steve would see me try to drink my problems away. I was chasing my rookie season, that fabulous campaign when I caught 80 balls and played like a Hall of Famer. I plummeted to 32 catches my second season and tried to find answers inside a bottle.

Of course, the booze never worked like I wanted it to work, which was to take away all the disappointment I was feeling of not duplicating my rookie season. The alcohol only made things worse. I began not to care because the pressure was building up. I covered it up with long nights out partying in an attempt to find some peace in my life. Many people might find this lifestyle attractive, but it was not at all. From the outside looking in, people would call it "ballin'," or doing it big. From the inside out, I was "BAWLING," doing it all wrong! All the while, Steve stood by my side making sure I got home safely.

Steve saw what was on the outside, not what was in my heart and soul. He did not see me crying on my knees begging God to give my life back, to give me a sense of peace, or at least some understanding of why I was experiencing this pressure in my life. It was supposed to be fun and games. I would pray for a new spirit, the strength to do things God's way and the power to take a stand for Him and stop doing things my way. I wanted to stop, but I was not spiritually strong enough to break the shackles that the world of fame, money and pride had on me.

While I was trying to gather myself and find some peace, Steve wanted to have his own things and his own money so that he could provide this type of lifestyle for himself, his friends and his family. Steve would eventually do whatever it took to get what he wanted even if he risked going to jail; he just wanted the so-called "life."

I met up with Steve one Thursday night when I flew into Baton Rouge. It was May 2011 and we sat down in a music studio and discussed how we were going to help a local boxer Justin. That was the last time I saw my bro because two days later I got another one of those calls, the calls you dread. It was Steve who had called me about

Marquis. Now the phone call, the doom, came from someone else... about Steve. I was so wrapped in my problems; I missed the warning signs about Steve.

It was a Saturday morning and "The Prince" was found dead along a deserted road in St. James Parrish. Word is a lot of people have committed suicide along this road. But he allegedly locked himself inside his vehicle and committed suicide. All the pressures of wanting to be happy, wanting to achieve "THE LIFE," or was it all of the pressure of consequences he was going to face for things he had done. Something he was truly ashamed of came crashing down that Friday night when he parked the car, rolled up the windows, locked the doors, and shot himself.

Still in all I blamed myself for Steve's death because I had the chance to give Steve some of the strength I had been building up inside me. Instead, I let my selfish desires shine brighter than God's spirit in me. I had a negative influence on my bro. I was not there, and I felt I helped cause this tragedy. I remember I was so mad that he would take his own life; I refused to allow myself to cry at all for the first few days. I also remember the day I broke down and sobbed. Finally, I was able to see the big picture.

I made a vow that day that everyone I met from then on would see the God in me over the ME in me. This was a tough time for Steve's friends and me, but one thing is certain, his death was not in vain. I became spiritually strong and transparent. I let God in my life, totally allowing Him to use me as a vessel to make others spiritually strong. With all my flaws, God was finally able to use me as he wanted. I was finally where I, deep down in my heart, wanted to be.

TRAGEDY IS A TEACHER

Steve's death taught me many lessons and 3 years after Steve's death, I still use those valuable lessons today and strive to make myself better. I have learned to be transparent and let people know who I am and what I stand for. I never know who is watching. That does not mean I act a different way and try and fool people. It means that I do not know who I could be hurting if I am not carrying myself appropriately. Why did I not see Steve's pain? Why did not I call Marquis more often? I learned that lesson the hard way with Marquis. I would advise anyone not to wait; pick up the phone because tomorrow is not promised. Check on a friend the minute the person crosses your mind, unless you are driving of course.

Our lives are daily lessons to draw us closer to God. We are all different, so it is inevitable that God teaches us in many different ways. I realize there is a lesson in everything we do, right or wrong, good or bad; and sometimes these lessons come at the price of a life. Let someone else's consequence be your teacher. Be willing and motivated to learn these lessons because they are like pieces to a puzzle. What do you want your finished product to be like?

"THE JOCK'S" LESSONS ON LOVE

Love Will Have Its Perfect Timing

At the age of 23 and in the NFL, I thought I was ready for the type of love that is required in a marriage. I did not understand what love really was. My wife was so amazing in my eyes that I married her after knowing her for just six months. She had no flaws, but I, on the other hand, had things to work on when it came to relationships. I thought that I knew how to make a woman happy, but as it turns out that I did not know anything. You see, sweet thoughts, flowers, cards and candies are sensitive and loving, until you hurt a woman's feelings or do something that you have no business doing. I realized that I needed to work on myself before I would begin to love a woman.

Before meeting my wife, like many young men, I felt like almost every pretty girl I met was "the one." Then I had to be real with myself and realize what was really making me feel that way. I would tell my male friends plenty of times, "Man this could be the girl. She is the ONE!", only to later learn that she was not the one at all. When I met my wife, it was something special, like right out of a movie. It felt like that tight gut feeling a person gets when asked to stand up in front of the class and present. During our six-month courtship, our lives played out like a chess game where every piece played its roll in order to secure the Queen. I had no doubt that she was the one for me from the moment I met her, but the question was if I was the one for her. My intuition would not let me stop thinking about her. My senses were going crazy so let me take you back to that moment August 2005.

It was my second year in the NFL and we had just played our last preseason game against the Miami Dolphins. Some of my friends were hosting a gathering at one of the local restaurants. I had just told my buddies Steve and Courtney that I was "cleaning out my closet" and that I was ready to settle down and find that one special woman. I even left them to go hang by myself so I would not have any distractions.

As I walked in the restaurant, there she was and I instantly sensed that she was different from the other women around her. She was the perfect picture, HD, everything else a blur. I did not know at the time, but she just so happened to be in town from medical school to visit her parents. I was thinking that she might be here to see some hot guy. I did not care though, all I knew was that this girl was smokin! As I was passing by her, I was gazing into her beautiful, soft brown eyes hoping she would look my way. She did so quickly, just as I expected. I remember thinking, "Rook to bishop, one point for me." I did not say a word; I just slipped right by and found the nearest table in the corner so I could post up, turn around, and see if she was still looking at me. When I did turn around she was still watching me. At that very moment, my friend Reese plops down at the table and said, "Man who you got your eyes on? I saw you looking from across the room". Just as I started to say, "Man who is that girl?" the Price Is Right music started playing in my head. All of a sudden I heard a young guy say, "Michael Clayton is that you? Man you have to meet this woman! Y'all would make a great couple!" Now I was thinking to myself, "What are you talking about?" As he continued to talk, I realized that he was referring to the same woman had my eye on. His words were like music to my ears and it sounded something like this:

Well the Girl over there you're starring at
could be your Queen for your life and that's a fact.
There were some questions in your mind like what is she about.
That's why I came over here to help you out.
There was a dude she dated back in the day.
He was the man back then-YO YO D-J.
But somewhere down the line, he did her wrong.
She packed her bags and to the left, she moved along.
Now she's standing in front of your very eyes.
The type of Dude you are-you could be her prize.
But you better hurry up cause it's the end of the song.
And the way she's lookin, she won't be there long.

Then the he disappeared POOF. Just like that, real talk. No lie. Well, it happened something like that.

As I am coming back to myself, my friend Reese looks at me and says "If you do not go talk to her, I will." That's when I thought, "Bingo! It was time to sacrifice my pawn to get close to the queen." Looking at her, I saw her staring back at me out of the corner of her eye. I mean, I was wrong to encourage such a bad idea, but no harm in him trying to talk to her. I told Reese, "Na Go ahead get your Mac on." He jumped out of his seat popped his collar and strutted right into the meat shop! Soon as he said hello in that, *I want you girl* voice, the woman cut him up with her eyes. He did not know what hit him. Pour little Reese. I quickly dashed across the room to try to catch her while she was still in her little "Diva" moment. "Why you do my friend like that," I said with a smile; "he just wanted to say hello." She looked at me and smiled as I thought to myself, checkmate-Queen down; I win! I patted Reese on the back "Thanks pawn you're dead and you can go. He laughed and took a loss for Team Clayton. As she and I danced the entire night, I think she knew that I was very interested in her. Only once did we separate the entire night. Before I could blink there was that guy out of nowhere again. "Did you like her? She is a good girl, yes? I told you she was wife material, oh and she is a doctor too." "For real," I thought silently. I would be lying if I told you I was not acting like a groupie, because I was, 100%. I was in love at first sight with Miss Wright.

I fell deeper and deeper in love, waste deep in love with finally the One! The real One! When the night was over I did not want to leave her side, but I kissed her on her forehead and told her goodnight. I told her she was going to be my wife that night just going off of my gut feeling. She smiled like "If you like it you better put a ring on it." I did put a ring on it and she has been by my side faithfully for seven years since.

Even though everything felt right with my wife, I still needed to grow. In a perfect world, I would have dated my wife a lot longer and grew outside of the marriage. Instead, I rushed and married her after only six months. The great thing was that I found an honest, loving, long-suffering wife that was able to deal with me throughout the years. The challenging part was growing and maturing inside of my marriage. It took me some time to mature and become the man she really deserved. I know I hurt her at times and let her down, and all I can say is that I was still growing. Had I just let love run its course, maybe I could have avoided some of the mistakes I made and some of the tears I caused by being insensitive and selfish. Instead, we etched our own path - a short cut so to speak - and at times in our relationship this was evident.

Many days I reflected on the choices my wife and I made early on. At times I was bothered because she was in medical school and on her way to fulfilling her dream of becoming a doctor. I fell in love with her and everything she represented. We moved really quickly and made some decisions in our lives that we could have done differently.

She would end up finishing her studies, but not her residency. This made it impossible for her to become a practicing doctor. Instead, we fell in love and started our family. My life intersected with hers, and love, in an ever so tender and loving way, derailed her from her lifelong dream. Still, it was a beautiful thing my wife and I were able to create. Timing just would not allow her to follow her dreams at this particular moment. Since we were meant to be together and truly believed that was what God had in store for us, no one could take it away and things still worked out. I am not saying that we did not have to fight tooth and nail to work out some of our issues, because we did. It was challenging at times. It still is to this very day. But any challenge is worth conquering when you love someone as I do my wife.

Five years later Tina would not only go back to college and get her MBA, but would be accepted back into a residency program. I am retired now and after eight long years in the NFL, our roles have changed. I am the one home with the kids - fixing plates and washing baby bottoms - and she is basically my sugar momma! The resilience she showed as she put countless hours into getting her MBA, the fortitude she displayed when she volunteered her time and talent to regain her confidence in being a doctor, the aptitude she had to step right back into the medical field after sitting out for five years without blinking an eye, shows that she is a courageous woman. She amazes me every day and I love her for that. I am truly a blessed man. Things turned out to be better than we expected, but the truth of the matter is that love still caused a bit of a setback.

Through my experience, I have learned that most times we make emotional decisions and we do not even think about what is affecting our choices at that time. It is important to always gather yourself and make a rational decision. Life in general is tough enough; why complicate things even more? Things tend to work out the way they are supposed to in the end, so do not add stress to your life with worry. Remember, we can create some obstacles for ourselves when we rush things. So take time to learn love and hope that you can see it when it crosses your path.

RECOGNIZE THE DIFFERENCE BETWEEN LOVE AND THE IDEA OF LOVE

The drama of TV fools us all. We see the instant infatuations on TV and the glamour of romance and we go looking for that lifestyle. Even in elementary school, kids find someone to call boyfriend or girlfriend and they have no idea what they are talking about. Everything is based on the idea of love. It is not so innocent when this puppy love turns into premarital sex at 14, 15, 16, and suddenly there is a baby. Lives are turned upside down when something that seemed to be a fun and innocent idea, becomes a harsh hunting reality.

Many people want to be able to say that they have a boyfriend or girlfriend and forget about the things that really matter in a relationship, such as trust, respect, and an active relationship with God. This is the difference between true love and the idea of love. Love is more than just saying it or liking the way a person looks, talks or walks. Love is highly present even if you couldn't see them.

When the phrase "love conquers all" is used, it means ALL! When one has real love for someone, they tend to do things that are sometimes not good for themselves. They will self-sacrifice and put others first for the sake of love. If the timing is not right, love has the power to get in the way of a person's hopes and dreams. It has the power to derail an individual from their purpose in life. This is why it is important not to get caught up in the Idea of Love. Love itself is tough enough to find, decipher, and secure, so do not play games with love.

A person might wonder, "When is a good time for love?" Well, I'll tell you that if you do not have a job, your own place, your own car, a college education or a career, and some goals for the future, then it is just too early for love. You better be able to take care of yourself before you start thinking about taking care of someone else. A lot of hearts are broken because people rush into a relationship. Trust me when I tell you, please do not rush it. Enjoy your life and when it is time for love, you will know it because you won't be able to run from it. I fell easy for love and in most cases it was the idea of love. What I found was, not only was I wasting mine, along with someone else's time, but I was complicating my life with things that would never take precedence. I did not understand how to love until I knew what love was.

DO NOT LET INFATUATION FOOL YOU

I remember meeting a young woman in college who was the sexiest girl I had seen at the time. She had the perfect hair, eyes, and skin. She was a complete package as far as looks are concerned. I remember everything I felt about love was magnified because I had never talked to a woman so pretty much more, made her my girlfriend. I knew deep down it was the beauty that had me trapped but I was still willing to see if other sparks would fly. We had a great time together, we grew to be really good friends. She was the only person at the time I would let my one year old daughter, Madison, see me with because I felt that she earned that much. We "played house" as they call it and carried ourselves as if we were married, or something close to it. What I thought was EROS love, or love restricted to one man, one woman relationships, was actually feelings lust and infatuation. I spent a year and a half getting to know her and there was still never anything major that stuck out to me that would make her that ONE! She probably was saying the same about me. I still continued to allow myself to be caught up in a physical attraction love flurry. I did whatever it took to keep this physical attraction going. I gave her money, let her use my apartment, truck, scooter, and tutors. Whatever she needed she had, just as long as she stood by my side and looked pretty. Sad thing is I did not want anything else in return. Then, I got drafted into the NFL and when I thought this would make it better it only exposed the truth. When you are a young single athlete, you are either on every woman's radar or trying to be. There seems to be some stigma with dating an athlete because a lot of times our reasons for dating are superficial: looks, chest and waste size, and sex.

As I started to meet other people, I realized there was nothing special about this woman that made her different from the others. They all were beautiful, nice to me, and cooked. Just when I got the feeling that maybe she and I needed to talk about where we wanted the relationship to go, I get a call from a guy I went to middle school with. "Hey BRO just thought you want to know your girl tried to holla at me at the Bayou Classic." Wow, really? I could not believe it. He even set up a three-way call so I could hear for myself. Just like that, after all that time, I never spoke to her again. Looking back at what was instant gratification then, evolved into one big waste of time, emotion, lunch and gas money. The monetary things I gave, the status of me becoming a NFL star, the physical attraction, none of it mattered. The only thing that mattered was that I could not grow the type of love needed to sustain in this relationship. In this adverse case it was "on to the next one", but not without the understanding that infatuation is not love.

Who wants to let go of real love; it is not something trivial that a person can move on from the very next day, regardless of the circumstance.

I have dated my share of beautiful women and they have all taught me something very important, beauty is not skin deep. Just because you are attracted to someone and everything seems good on the outside, it does not necessarily mean that things will be flawless on the inside. For all the men reading, please know that a woman may be beautiful on the outside, but if she does not have a heart of gold and good morals nothing else matters. Do not set a relationship up for failure. For ladies, it does not matter if a man has muscles and is tall and handsome. If he does not demonstrate respect and dignity in the relationship, then do not bother to stick around to see if it will grow organically. Either a man has it or not. I believe a person should have high standards and should never compromise their core values to be in a relationship even if the other person has the potential to make a lot of money.

Love is a commitment that you must make and stick to as long as the other person is doing his or her part. I had to learn the hard way that not everyone who looks good *to* you is good *for* you. A person needs to have beautiful qualities on the inside instead of only on the outside in order for you to truly love them.

DO NOT CHANCE IT

While waiting for the right person, focus on loving yourself. If you do not respect yourself, how can one respect another person? It is a software/hardware issue. The computer, you, is a sparkling machine with the fastest processor. But if the software (your mindset and work ethic) is faulty, the computer does not run well. Here is what else is important. Before one can love someone unconditionally, they have to know what they want to accomplish in life and have a plan for them. Most times, achieving that plan requires hard work and being a bit selfish. It requires working 16-hour days and working weekends and perhaps some travel. How much of that should a mate get subjected to?

The secret is to respect self first and use it as a foundation. Work from that foundation and real love will come naturally. A lot of times, we try to have a relationship before we truly love ourselves. Loving someone should not derail an individual's personal goals or unnecessarily complicate an individual's life. Love will work itself out if given enough time. Love can be a great thing, but if you do not love yourself first, it could become your worst nightmare. The plans you have for your life might not be someone else's plans for you, and they could ruin your plans. Also, because not everyone knows how to love, some relationships are full of pain and agony. I have seen people lose scholarships because they were too caught up in a toxic relationship.

I almost rejected my college football scholarship because I had a child on the way and felt the need to work and support my family. I felt the idea of love and starting a family was more honorable than playing football. I needed to be responsible. I was wrong because I was not ready for my daughter. The power of love was so strong I needed my closest friends to convince me that continuing on my path of sports was the best decision I could make at that time. If it were not for them, I most definitely would have had to live with regret beyond all understanding. My daughter Madison is twelve now and lives in Houston with her mother, and I only see her during summer and on holidays. I still remember taking her to classes with me at LSU. I was so young I did not even know how to properly ask for help.

My daughter and I have a great relationship, but there are so many things I could have done better. I set a standard for myself to keep up a relationship with her and call her and stay in touch and let her know, without doubt, I was her dad.

I have seen people flunk out of school because their grades became too low over a relationship they were too caught up in. I have seen people go to jail because they were *too* into a relationship. That is when the relationship begins to ruin the lives of both people. Instead of sharing love between two people, what is truly felt is hate and lust, so the two people end up ruining each other.

Being a parent is the hardest job in the world especially if you are a kid yourself. Imagine this:

One day a teenager wakes up . . . and he is a father. How daunting is that? No job and I was a father. I was still in school and a father. Over and over I said one thing to myself: "dumb."

I was a freshman in college and was becoming a father. If you want something to get in the way of your dreams, this can do it- unprotected sex. I was too young, and my child's mother was too young. We did not know what we were doing. The social pressures and the moment itself overwhelmed us. We did not love each other, so I knew that we would not be happy trying to start a life together.

Growing up in the South where people tend to have many traditional values, there were quite a few of my peers who decided to remain abstinent. Through them, I was able to see how much easier my life would have been had I waited. Believe it or not, I played alongside some virgins in the NFL and it was amazing to see their strength. Because they were not sexually active, they had a totally different focus than other players. Of course, you hear about Tim Tebow publicly, but there are quite a few more virgins in the NFL. They were the smart ones. Imagine trying to get your career on track as a player in the NFL and worrying about whether the child you have fathered is taken care of. Who is home to watch over them when the mother is just a woman you met by chance one night?

The men who were abstinent did not have to worry about entertaining several women at once. More importantly, they did not have to worry about the child they helped create. There is envy in the NFL for those players who could keep temptation at arm's length. It is a difficult thing to do because as an athlete, you have money. You are a target. Those players that chose to remain abstinent did not have to worry about being up into the early hours of the morning talking to or trying to woo women all of the time. They did not have to miss practice or accidentally oversleep because they spent their nights hanging out too much with women. They were able to focus on the task at hand. Some of the men were not as talented as others, but they were able to make it to the NFL and stay there because of their focus.

I knew guys who stayed home because they got a girl pregnant instead of going to college and most of those guys never reached their full potential in life. The responsibility of being a parent can overwhelm a teenager.

Coach Saban knew about me becoming a father and supported me. He wanted me there at LSU so I had to make it work. I would tell myself every day, "I gotta be successful; I have a little girl depending on me." I would get up every morning before class and run a mile before I went to go lift weights. I ran with my daughter in mind and she is what pushed me towards greatness. When others were sleeping, I was working. I saw a finish line in my mind and knew that I had to get there.

In college, I decided to work harder than everyone around me. I decided that I couldn't lie down and accept defeat. I would wake up in order to change my daughter's diapers in the middle of the night only to wake up once again a few hours later to train. All of this just to stay focused and make a better life for her. I worked as if I was already getting paid to play football. Do not get me wrong, I had the best times of my life in college, but I worked even harder because of my daughter, Madison. I did my best to not let anything come between football, me, and my little girl.

On top of that, because I was the big man on campus, my daughter's mother started having problems with me. It was a huge responsibility being a father in college and trying to balance fatherhood, school, football, the college life. It was a juggling act that could easily make someone fail. I thank God that I made it through.

Because I loved my daughter with all my heart, she inspired and motivated me to be better. She was my driving force every day in college. I was doing all that I could so that she would have a better life; it was all for her. Like many things in life, with the good comes the bad. A sad thing is that I couldn't always be there for her because her mom was not the one for me. I even went to the lengths of trying to marry her mom because I felt every child deserves to have both of their parents in the home as I did, but it just did not work out between us. So we couldn't raise our daughter in the same home like a traditional family. That was tough, but it became my reality.

I have to be honest about this situation and say it was not the way I planned it and I would not wish that on anyone or any child. I was lucky enough to be raised in a two-parent home, so not being able to have that for my daughter was tough for me. Once I left for the NFL, I prayed every day that my two-year old daughter would know that her daddy loved her. She was so young and innocent. Then, in the blink of an eye, Madison was twelve years old. I have found that the older she gets, the more she misses me and the more she misses me, the more Madison is hurt that we are apart. I created this situation long ago, and as a father who deeply cares for his child, I will always feel like I have to make up for lost time. I have to face my reality and continue to do the best that I can for her. I saw my own father go through the same situation because he became a parent while in college, and I always thought he set a great example of how to remain committed to your children no matter what.

I'm thankful for my upbringing because I probably would have thrown in the towel and quit before I even started, had I not been raised to hold family in high regard. I had to make things work with the consequences that I had brought upon myself. Now, I realize that not everyone will become a pro athlete and not everyone has the fortune of being brought up by two parents; nevertheless, I believe that we all have the ability to make good choices. My dad lost his father to cancer and was forced to find a way to bring up his children properly, with love and respect for others. He was successful in doing so because he chose to be. My goal is to be better than my father and for my kids to be better than me. This takes love, patience, wisdom, and most importantly, I believe the power of God.

ABSTAIN IF AT ALL POSSIBLE

Save yourself until you know without a shadow of a doubt that you are with the person that you want to marry and spend the rest of your life with. If you cannot say that about them, then it is too early to be having sex. You should wait.

I believe sex is for adults. Today, more and more teens are getting into sexual activities and getting pregnant or catching sexually transmitted diseases (STDs). The world is much more dangerous than it used to be. Statistics say that up to 85% of people will catch an STD in their lifetime. Who wants to be in that number? If you are honest with yourself, the main reason you want to be sexually active is most likely because it seems that everyone else is doing it. You probably feel like you would be left out and made fun of if you did not indulge as well.

Well, guess what? By waiting until marriage, you will be the one who will get the last laugh. There is nothing fun about being a parent before or at the age of 18. It could break you down and change your life for the worse. Yes, you will love the child, and it will be a blessing in every sense if you allow it to be, but it could also spoil your dreams if you are not cautious. You have to make sure that you are smart about this. Before you do anything sexually, you have to ask yourself what you would do if the worst-case scenario happened. What would you do if you caught an STD? What would you do if you brought a baby into the world? How would you take care of yourself? How would you take care of your child? Those are some serious questions that you have to ask yourself.

It will mean so much more to the person that you marry if you save yourself for them. They will feel special and so much closer to your heart. Saving yourself will also please your parents and God. Do not be afraid to be different. The world needs more leaders, and leaders are not afraid to be different from the crowd.

THE ROAD TO THE NFL: EARN YOUR KEEP

The World Is Not Set Up for You to Succeed

Misery was just one drug deal away. Misery was breaking in someone's car and stealing. Misery was an alcohol binge, a fight, an angry push in the hallway or back talk to a teacher. Misery was sleeping in, skipping school, failing grades. Misery was at my fingertips growing up every step of the way.

I would see guys that were from my part of Baton Rouge, guys that I knew, guy's with talent just like me – and they got trapped by the misery of too many false steps. Drugs, women, alcohol, bad grades, and crime were part of the numerous one- man crime waves all over town.

I was able to navigate around all of it but some days, I barely made it. The temptation to do wrong will come at you over and over. I was foolish to think it was cool to stay out late, miss school at times, and find some girls to hang out with. Boys in high school do not know any better; and

I made some mistakes. Some serious enough that it could have ruined my dreams of playing major D-1 college football. I was just lucky not to get caught, and even luckier to finally make a conscious decision to straighten my act up and fly right.

I gave in to the peer pressure countless times, like making a baby, but I survived. That was I; I was a survivor. My successes and triumphs were, in large part, thanks to my parents helping to steer me away from the consequences of bad behavior. I was able to sign a Division 1 scholarship, whereas other guys were not so lucky. Misery hit them right in the face-the same misery that was looking to take me out. The main lesson that I learned is that you have to show some discipline. People are not going to throw rose petals at your feet because they will be too busy throwing stones instead. A few of my friends participated in the same troublesome things I used to do, and as you might expect, things did not turn out the way that they wanted it to. Some of them missed out on the opportunity to go to college, get an education, and play ball. This lead to what I saw as a path of destruction.

When I got to college and I had some status in my community as a D-1 football player. I realized I could not be a knucklehead and make any bad choices because people were watching me. I saw the influence that I had on others and never reverted back to the trouble that I used to find in my earlier years. My goals took over and beat back temptation. I wanted to help my football team at LSU become the best team in the country, but I realized that I could not do this by participating in things that could cost me my career. It was so refreshing to have my teammates look up to me and coaches looked to me to be the example. This is what cool should have been seen as: being a leader that people depend on to do the right thing. Having the strength to overcome life's temptations felt like winning a big-time football game.

If you want to be seen as "The Man" or "The Woman", then you had better start acting like it, not some punk player who thinks things are going to be handed to him. Discipline is what propelled me into being one of the top players in the country and one of the best all-around players in LSU's history.

I am sure many young people face the same pressures I faced as a young man in some form or another. The "negative influencers" is what I called them. It can be your friends encouraging you to cheat on a test, the peer pressure to start having sex, music that influences you to rebel against your parents, sagging your pants, smoking weed, drinking alcohol, or taking a short cut in school. With such influences all around, it can appear that life is one big roller-coaster with a sign at the end that says, "We hope you fail, have a nice day!" Teenagers are faced with hundreds of problems and I believe the best solution is discipline. With discipline you can and will overcome anything that life puts in your path. Remember, it is a choice that only you have the power to apply. Do so and you will surly get the most out of your opportunities in life.

HAVE A PLAN

The world is not some private playground for you to own. It sets parameters for you. One of those parameters is that life is not going to hand you a free ride. You have to work for it. Go get what you want. Do not wait for someone to make a plan for you. You have to realize that the choice to better yourself is in your hands, no matter how old or young you are. You have to find the strength to choose the right path for your life. That path is not going to come from a rapper with the hidden messages of rebellion and easy money. This is not a life plan that will last. Following their words is a good way to end up in jail, passed over for a job, ignored on the football field even. Where will that rapper be then? Where will the guy who taught you that being a rebel was the way to live your life be when you need some good advice? He is not going to be shelling money out for you. No, he will be moving on to the next sucker who is enticed by fast cars and fast women.

The magazine that promoted the flamboyant lifestyle, the movie that showed the gangsters as heroes will all seemingly take you down the wrong path. That is someone else's destructive plan. Leave it be. Media is saturated with these lifestyles of the rich and famous and all the grandeur that comes with money. Success can be in the palm of your hands, but it is not going to come with a shortcut. You need a plan. You must plan, prepare, and take action to succeed.

PLEASURE CAN BE PAINFUL

No matter what decision you are facing, look at the consequences. Can you see that far ahead? Try. If the end result of your action is something that you will regret, do not do it. It may seem fun in the moment and may bring you some pleasure, but pleasure does not always lead to happiness. Pleasure can also lead to pain.

Drinking alcohol may bring pleasure, but eventually it will bring pain when your kidneys fail you or you get behind the wheel of a car and cause an accident. Smoking weed may bring pleasure, but eventually it will bring pain when you fail a drug test and lose your job or move on to more serious drugs. Having sex outside of marriage may bring pleasure, but eventually it will bring pain if you catch an STD or have a baby too young.

The prison system is counting on you. The government has allowed prisons to fall into the hands of corporations who make money off of your mistakes. Why do you want to put more money into someone else's pocket? So many people are incarcerated and treated like gangsters when their crime was simple possession of marijuana. While children of people with money get off with suspended sentences and picking up roadside trash, the others, many black kids, get locked up. The prisons do not care. You will shower and dine along with murderers. All it takes is a little dope and you become part of the money making machine. In many municipalities now, the new car driven by the sheriff came from the proceeds of finding that dime bag in the car and then being able to seize a car because it was being used in a crime. In this world you have to learn how to avoid these types of pitfalls.

Earn your keep by what? Not waiting until you're ready? No!

Abortion clinics are racking in millions from teenagers making poor decisions and then cannot deal with the consequences.

Earn your keep by what? Doing things that get you locked up? No!

Drugs do nothing but take you further away from your hopes, dreams and goals. Drugs ruin lives, neighborhoods, families, relationships and everything else they come in contact with.

Earn your keep by what? Being a person who puts drugs in your body or into the streets? No!

Earn your keep by choosing to be successful- choosing to be your very best self- yes!

TAKE ACTION ON YOUR PLANS

Goals: Set life goals: one-year goals, two-year goals, five-year goals or even ten-year goals.

Plan: Make a goal achievement plan. Ask someone who has experienced a similar situation or go the library and do some research on the identified goals. Mentors are available everywhere. They are in your church, local community center, and even at your school. Stay behind after the church service is over and ask a church member questions like: What do you do for a living? How did you grow your interest in that profession? How much money can I make? Pick up some tips from success stories around you, local businesses, and professionals in your neighborhood. Be active in your success. Everything needed to be great is right in front of anyone who is willing to go get it.

Action: After you have decided that you want to succeed, you have to take action. It is not enough to simply write your goals down. You have to move towards them and stick to what you said you wanted to do. It will not be easy, but it will be worth it.

Do not expect things to be easy or to fall into your lap. Be ready to work hard for what you want in life. It will pay off for you if you stay focused and stay disciplined. Will you practice patience? Can you put in the time? One of the most significant pieces of advice that I can give young people is to be careful of what you listen to and what you watch. You never know where a message you hear or see will take you. A lot of times it will take you somewhere you do not want to go and have you doing things you do not want to do. It will cost you more than you're willing to pay. Do your very best to stay on the path to success. Life will try to derail you from your path at every corner. Recognize these obstacles and get out of the way! Be strong and do not go astray.

One of the best remedies for staying on the true path is to find allies, who share the same dreams and aspirations, because there is strength in numbers. When temptation starts to build up and feel as if it might get the best of you, a good friend will always help rationalize the situation.

DO NOT TAKE SHORT CUTS

At LSU, we went from being the Southeastern Conference champions during my freshman year (9-3) when we won the Western Division, to a roller-coaster season my sophomore year when we finished third in the Western Division. Even though we had some down times that year, we also won one of the greatest comeback victories in college history. We won the Bluegrass Miracle, a last chance and last grasp win at Kentucky. This was a moment in LSU's history that fans, coaches and players will never forget. This was also the most memorable moment that really taught me the most about not taking short cuts in life and always giving your very best effort.

We were beating the University of Kentucky in the third quarter, 21-7. The truth is that we should have dominated more, but the other team was willing to fight to the end. Devery Henderson, (a 9 year veteran receiver for the New Orleans Saints), was on his way to having the biggest game in his collegiate career. We were starting to coast through the game thinking we had it in the bag, but then the crap hit the fan. Coach Saban's mindset since we stepped on campus was to never think we had won the game until it was over, but we forgot all about that discipline in the second half. Kentucky came back at us with their hefty quarterback, Jared Lorenzen, pitching the ball all over the field. We kept making one small mistake after another allowing the Wildcats the opportunity to claw their way back into the game. The lackadaisical mindset had crept in and we could not shake it. We had tried to take a short cut to a win and, because of that, we were about to get embarrassed.

The University of Kentucky took a 30-27 lead with 25 seconds to play on a field goal. We were deflated. I will never forget the feeling of defeat taking over the sideline. We knew that we had fallen victim to taking short cuts and not giving our very best effort, which put us in a no-win situation. Just as we had fallen trap to celebrating prematurely and being overly confident, on the other sideline, the Kentucky players dumped the traditional Gatorade shower on the head coach Guy Morris in celebration of what they believed was an inevitable win. He, wisely, was not happy about that because he knew that the game was not over.

Their celebration was already underway across the field. The fans were jumping over the stadium railing, taking over the sidelines ready to storm the field. They anticipated one of Kentucky's greatest comeback victories, a victory over the mighty LSU tigers. Kentucky kicked the ball off to the dangerous Henderson, who had scored two touchdowns on the day already. He unselfishly sprinted forward only gaining a few yards before running out of bounds to preserve as much time on the clock as possible. To make matters worse, on the opening play of this final drive, we got a delay of game penalty. We were sloppy the entirety of the second half.

With only about 20 seconds left on the clock, and backed up inside of our own 10-yard line, there were only a few plays we had to choose from. All season we had practiced situational football, and Coach Saban would give the offense approximately one minute and forty five seconds to go the full length of the field. To go more than 90 yards in 25 seconds seemed impossible at this point. We were on our 8-yard line.

After how we had played in the second half, you would not think that we had a chance; but there was still time on the clock. There was still time for us to come alive and "play hard for 60 minutes," which was a saying that Coach Saban drilled into our heads. Win or lose, we knew we should play hard for 60 minutes. I can remember quickly thinking that I did not want to be the one called out in the meeting room for slacking on the last few plays in a losing effort. We were already on the verge of a verbal lashing by Coach Saban about our performance in the first half. So I made sure to finish hard, no shortcuts. We all did. Marcus Randall, our quarterback, brought the play into the huddle, "all go Z in". I was the Z receiver on this play so I knew the ball was coming to me. We lined up in a four-receiver set, three receivers on the right side and one receiver on the left. All of the receivers would run verticals to get the defense out of the middle of the field, and the Z receiver would run a 20-yard in route. As Marcus said "Hut!" I was not only sprinting for my 20-yard depth, but I was also looking at the clock tick away. I was 15 yards downfield and felt that I needed to start my break early because, at this point, only 7 seconds were left on the clock. Marcus fired a low ball to me across the middle for a 17-yard gain. I slid to make the catch, and then popped up to quickly to call a time out with only 2 seconds remaining on the clock. We only had one play to call as the offense gathered on the sideline. This was not just a Hail Mary situation; this was "the" Hail Mary situation. It was not so much of a situation, really, but was more of a predicament. Usually in practice we would throw the ball into the end zone from the 50-yard line. We were 75 yards away. It never worked from 50 yards out, so the question was "how it was supposed to work from 75 yards out." No one knew what we were about to encounter, especially the Kentucky fans who were ready to storm the field.

Marcus brought the second play into the huddle and told us, "dash right 93 Berlin." We lined up in the same formation as the play before. This would be the last play of the game, which also meant that it gave us one last chance to give it all we had. The ball was snapped around our 25-yard line, and the only thing that was on my mind was to run hard and fast. I started outside with the assignment of being the deep guy and Devery started inside of me being the tip guy. As we weaved through defenders 50 yards down field, all of us ended up in the wrong spots. However, because we did not take short cuts in practice, even if we knew it would not work, we paid attention to each other's assignments, so we made the adjustment during the play. I became the jump guy at the last second as the ball came down, and Devery became the deep guy.

As the ball approached, I did my best to tip it to Devery, coming within inches of touching it, but I missed. The only thing I accomplished was distracting the defender from catching an interception. He should have just knocked the ball down. Then, the blue grass miracle happened. The distracted defender misjudged the height of the throw and it bounced off his pads right into Devery's hands in full stride. Devery ran through a few of Kentucky's fans, which thought they were celebrating a win. There were even fans hanging from the goal posts. Devery raced to the end zone and the whole Commonwealth of Kentucky was absolutely stunned. To tell you the truth, we all were.

Being stunned only lasted for a second for us because when you are on the winning side, joy overtakes you immediately. Tears of joy and relief began to flow and the reality of taking shortcuts was imprinted in my brain forever. I learned that when the odds are next to impossible, good things could still happen so never ever give up; and stay away from shortcuts.

THE NFL DRAFT

I am sure that this is the part of my story everyone really wants to know; "What happened after my rookie season with the Bucs?" A few of you may even have purposely skipped to this section, without understanding my entire journey and knowing a little bit about what I have been through. If you did skip to this section, go back at some point and read the previous chapters!

My rookie season started off in a strange way because my best friend, Ike, was in a bad car accident the day before I had to report to the Tampa Bay Bucs. Let me take you back to that day.

As I rolled up to Ike's white Camaro, it felt like I was in a movie. The car was shattered into hundreds of broken pieces all over the street, like it had been through a shredder. Only minutes before, instead of riding together like we would always do, we decided to take separate cars. Tears began to fill my eyes as my hands began to shake and knees buckle. Stumbling out of the car in a panic, I slowly walked up to the car afraid to find my best friend dead inside. His head was bent back to the seat rest. "No Lord," I screamed in anguish. "NO." The white shirt he wore was fully covered with blood as even more continued to pour from his head and arms.

Ike was the first friend I ever had. We were like brothers; blood would not have made us any closer. Looking at him in that very moment was like watching a horror film in the flesh. With tears streaming down my face, I got a step closer as he reached his arm out of the window. I grabbed his hand not knowing what to do. I was frozen for a quick second. Sarcastically, Ike looked at me and said, "So you just gonna sit there and watch me die? Negro, get me out of here!"

Even in a critical moment like this, I found joy that my friend still possessed his sense of humor. I did everything that I could to pry the door open, but it resembled more of a smashed tin can, a crumpled up mess, than anything like a car door. As he sat there, his legs smashed and broken, bleeding profusely from head to toe, I held his head up and kept him awake until the ambulance arrived. It took the Jaws of Life to rip open the car and pull him out. He had been trapped in that car 45 minutes.

This was such a tragic event in my life because ever since we were six years old, Ike and I had dreams of making it big: big in sports, big in Hollywood, big in whatever. As long as we were big in something, Ike was satisfied. I remember spending the night at each other's houses every weekend. We would wake up at five in the morning, sneak out the house and jog around the block.

We were only six years old, but we both felt like we were destined for greatness.

We were together as kids and we were together in the hospital. I was scheduled to leave the next day for training camp and Ike was supposed to go with me, but he was in a coma because of the head trauma. We had made it so far together; now I was faced with having to leave my best friend behind on, what seemed to me at the time, as his deathbed.

Ike was in a coma for two weeks after I left. Every day after camp, I wrote him a letter. I would tell him what I did that day, what my goals were and what I was going to do during my rookie season. I let this tragedy inspire me to dominate because I wanted the best stories in those letters. I wanted Ike to be proud. I would send my letters to Ike's mom, who would read them to him beside his hospital bed. She would call and tell me that he could not talk, but he heard her and responded in his own way. She knew he could hear her and he was listening to the stories.

Ike was the reason that I worked so hard during my rookie season; I dedicated that season to him. The motivation that I had when the season started may be the reason that I played so well. That momentum carried on for 16 weeks. It felt like Ike was on my shoulder, always acting as my rock to keep me grounded and focused. It turned out that my rookie season was the best season of my NFL career, by far. I had 80 receptions, 1,193 yards, and 7 touchdowns that year. I was the talk of the NFL. From then on, I would forever chase my rookie year.

What happened? Life happened; the NFL happened. After the 2004 season was over, the Tampa Bay team doctors told me I needed minor knee surgery. This was new to me because I had never needed surgery before. My body had always bounced back after a little rest. Sure, my knee was sore, but that happens in football. You rest, you give your body time to heal and then you bounce back. At least that was the way it was in college. The NFL was no different. Staple it, sow it, and screw it back together if you have to, just get me back on the field. Now in the NFL there are mini-camps, OTA's, and off-season workouts, the kind that are mandatory/optional. That meant that you did not have to show up, but you had better be there or else. The problem was that the older you get the slower your body responds. In the Bucs case they did try to give me a chance to heal on my own but it was taking too long. Missing all the prep work for the season due to injury, I decided to go under the knife because it ensured a more detailed plan for recovery. By then it was too late. I had already missed the off-season, and recovery time seemed to get me back for training camp. My knee was still jacked up when training camp rolled around and that caused a rift between my head coach, Jon Gruden, and me. I did not understand the tension between him and I because I got hurt giving him my all. Every time he looked at me, it was with these disappointed, accusatory eyes. It almost felt like he was saying, "It is your fault you're not out here, Clayton."

I hung my head because for the first time, I was unable to please my coach on any level. I honestly wanted to please everyone: my coach, my newfound fans from my rookie season, my family and my friends. Now, I was injured for the first time in my career and there was a serious sense of a loss of self-esteem. One thing led to another and there were reports in the media that I was in Gruden's "doghouse." What did I do to get there? I did not know. Who started these media rumors? I did not know, did not really care either. This was not football to me: this was a mind game or "The Business of Football", as they call it. All I knew was I could only control what I could control, which was rehabbing and trying to get back to being 100 percent healthy.

By the time training camp rolled around, I was almost ready. Camp would be the first time that my knee would get any real action. I was not where they wanted me to be and I suppose the ship sailed on anyway. Ike Hillard, a savvy, well-respected veteran, was brought in to be the 3rd down receiver. Joey Galloway was healthy to resume his number one spot, and I became an afterthought. The offense was struggling to keep guys healthy on the line and, more importantly, to find a starting quarterback. Of my six seasons with the Bucs, eleven quarterbacks took over as the starter, two of which started twice. This is never good for any receiver, let alone the number 2 or 3 receiver, but there was not that much I could do about it.

I slipped to 32 catches my second season in 2005, then 33 in 2006. The media judged me as if I was the number one guy. I wasn't even the number 2 guy. Ike Hillard got three times the amount of balls I got. I would have some long talks with Coach Gruden, some of which brought us both to tears. We were always able to reason within the confines of his office. He said he was trying to find the right quarterback and trying to get guys back healthy, for me to be patient and keep working hard. Maybe this was said because I had come to see him man to man. Deep down I always wanted to believe that after I got past his ego and his arrogance that he truly cared about me as player and a person. This did not prove to be true because soon I started to see what he would say about me in the papers and hear what he would say behind my back to coaches who respected me. I knew then what I was dealing with. I was a 22-year-old young man dealing with the pressures of the NFL and I was lost. Every day I had to find strength to pick myself up, look this man in the face every day and respect him because he was still my coach. Even though I felt that I had lost all respect for my head coach showing it was not an option. Other players had shown their frustration and it only made them look silly. Even if they were 100% correct. I respected the authority of the head coach and his title, but not his methods. I was losing respect for the game that I once loved because of pride, egos, negative press, and the business of football. I was losing respect for myself because I played on, kept quiet, and did not speak up.

I will never forget the day that I walked onto the practice field, and one of my coaches, who will remain nameless, said, "You better get your ass in gear because this draft I'm gonna get me some of those BIG, BLACK, STRONG NIGGERS." As shocking as this may seem, I had the same experience when I was a freshman at LSU. The only difference is that at LSU, I bashed that guy's nose in. I thank God for giving me the peace I needed to control myself because I would have seriously damaged my reputation and career had I reacted similarly with the Tampa Bay coach.

Still, I was bewildered and rubbed the wrong way. I would think to myself how comfortable he must be around me to say this to my face, trying to find a positive in what had happened. He grabbed my shoulder and said it with conviction. I did not say a word. I forced a grin and shook my head. Had it been any other time, I would have probably made sure that he thought twice about using that word again. I was disoriented because I wanted to be accepted again and have the opportunity to play the game the way that I knew I could play it. Sadly, I felt like I gave up my pride for the love of the game. To react the way that I wanted to in that moment would have led to the doom of my career in the Tampa organization which I still loved dearly.

It was a feeling of helplessness and it would have destroyed me completely if I had let it linger. I took the initiative from that point on to take every young player under my wing; I wanted to build them up to be solid men in every aspect of life. I did not know it at the time, but by doing this I was building myself back up as well. I did my best to lead by example so that the young men could learn to position themselves for success and stability. This meant becoming a true professional, the consummate pro. I made it a goal, to lead my teammates to carrying themselves in a professional manner. I made sure that I, at least, made a difference in this way. I honestly believe that

I found my purpose in helping others in this way because it brought me a peace that football never provided after my rookie season.

After five years with the Bucs, ownership decided to fire the majority of the staff and they ended up hiring from within. Mark Dominick, a long-time front office staffer, became the General Manager. He would come up to me on the plane after every away game and say, "Mike, I see what you are doing, keep working hard." Raheem Morris, the long-time defensive back coach, who had been a fan of mine since I played my first down as a Buccaneer, became the head coach. I had received a lot of negative press for not being as productive as I was during my rookie season. I was made a fool of publicly before my wife and loved ones. It did not matter that I made a conscious decision to put my teammates first and my career second, I was still ridiculed. But an amazing thing happened. The new staff thought that I had something left to give; it probably would not be 80 catches a season, but they saw some value in old Michael Clayton. Maybe it was my devotion to teammates off the field. In any case, the new staff rewarded me with a new contract worth more than $25 million. Not for catches, yards or touchdowns but for being a humbled leader.

NOT EVERYONE WILL BE A FAN

Even though this was such a defining moment in my life, there were still people who said I did not deserve a new contract and the Bucs were crazy for keeping me around.

Why could they not just be happy for me? I learned eventually that not everyone will be in your corner, no matter how good an individual you may be. There are people in this world who are jealous, so it is to be expected that they would react with scorn to my new deal. I worked hard. I did not lie down after my rookie year. The numbers did not go down because I coasted. I had to accept the criticism and control only what I knew that I could control.

DO NOT BECOME BITTER

People regularly ask me if I have any type of resentment for the things I went through with the Bucs. My answer... absolutely not. I made it through the fire and was better for it. Remember, it was the Bucs that drafted me and gave me a chance. Things did not go smoothly after my rookie season, but I am not resentful. They had faith in me again with another contract. I believe that resentment sets in when we allow ourselves to settle with circumstances or allow this evil world to have its way with us and we do not stand up to fight back.

Everything I learned in my six years with the Bucs prepared me for the next chapter in my life once I was released. I learned how to deal with adversity and setbacks. I took a job with the Omaha Nighthawks, in the United Football League. It was basically the minor leagues, but turned out to be the best thing that ever happened to me. I discovered who I really was in Omaha 2010. It was the lowest I have ever felt but I had been here before with the Bucs. The New York Football Giants stumbled upon me in Omaha and had heard that I still carried myself as if I was in the NFL. To me I was just trying to be great and control what I could control. To them it showed that I would fight for greatness no matter the circumstance. I earned a roster spot on that Giants football team that year and the following year which in 2011 we defeated Tom Brady and the Patriots in Super Bowl XLVI.

DO NOT BE AFRAID OF DIFFICULT TIMES

The world can be unforgiving at times. This is why you must know what *you* can control. Do your part at being your very best self. Allow your faith to lead you through tough, painful, and discouraging times. Trust and believe that, one day, Grace and Mercy will find you on your journey. When that happens, wounds will suddenly show themselves as accomplishments. You will see the wounds as badges of honor. You earned those, so do not be afraid to fail.

I was told a story once about some kids who loved to visit the silversmith shop. The most fascinating thing for them was the silver before it went into the fire. The silver was black, rusty, and just ugly; nothing similar to what you might expect silver to look like. The coal like substance would be placed into the fire and after a while, what seemed to be black coal began to change into the precious metal we know as silver. Now, if the silversmith left the silver in the fire too long, the silver would melt and be worthless. If he did not leave it in long enough, it would not reach its full potential value.

I know you are wondering right now, "Well, how does he know when to take the silver out?" I was saying the same thing when I heard the story. He takes the silver out of the fire when he can see a reflection of himself. Only then is it at its peak.

If you learn anything from this book, please understand the point that I am trying to make right now. We are all God's precious stones and He is our silversmith. He knows to take us out of the fire when He can see His reflection in us. Only then are we able to reach our full potential value. I tell this story to say, "Never be afraid of the fire."

LEARN TO RESPECT AUTHORITY

You are Not Doing Anything That They Have Not Done

I was fortunate to learn this valuable lesson growing up with both of my parents, Milton and Marjorie. I can remember when I was younger and I would often stay out past my curfew. I would stay out in order to see my girlfriend or hang out with Ike. Sometimes, I would come in before my curfew and then go back out. My favorite exits were the side porch, climbing out of windows and even jumping off the roof. I thought that I was onto something and had found a way to get around my parent's rules. After all, I was having fun in the moment and even getting a rush from avoiding detection.

One day, out of the blue, my dad said, "Look here boy, if you are going to leave the house, just go out the front door because you tearing up my darn window screen!" It turns out that I accidentally started to tear up the window screen trying to sneak out. My dad had his own way of telling me to stop doing what I was doing. I could have fallen over in shock when he said that. How did he know it was me? How did he know I was sneaking out and that the screen had not just gotten hit on accident? Looking back, my dad probably heard me some of those nights. He probably looked out of his window at me walking out of the driveway and just shook his head. He probably heard me sneaking back in, too. In fact, my dad probably did the same thing when he was young. Where I thought that I was pulling one over on my parents, my dad knew all along what I was doing. The fact was that he had much more life experience than I did, so I should have known that he was on to my tricks.

Since I am a parent now, I hope that I can get my kids to understand that I have been where they are going and if they listen to me, life will be much easier on them. I wonder if every parent and caretaker's wish is to make life easier for their children. Unfortunately, it does not always work out that way.

PARENTS AND AUTHORITY FIGURES KNOW MORE THAN YOU THINK

Parents, grandparents, teachers, pastors, coaches, caretakers and others in positions of authority have valuable lessons to share. I chose to focus on the term "authority" because not all children have parents, much less both parents raising them. You have to understand that people in authority are there for a reason. They have been through enough in life that, when the hammer comes down, they can teach kids a lesson. If you are a teenager reading this book, I want you to realize something. While you think that you are pulling one over on your parents, they probably know exactly what you are doing and are just watching you and waiting until the opportune moment to teach a lesson. To save yourself from embarrassment and punishment, you might just want to quit now. If your behavior has not caught up to you yet, it will. The consequences might not even come down on you from your parents. Those consequences might come from a police officer that is cuffing you or a coach putting you on the bench. Life is like that window screen I thought I was sneaking through-I was not as clever as I thought I was. For me, the lesson was waiting on the other side.

APPLY THE WISDOM AND ADVICE OF AUTHORITY FIGURES IN YOUR LIFE

If you are a young person, you will more than likely hit an age where you feel too cool for parents to be around or feel that they do not understand what you are going through. There is nothing new under the sun. Whether it is drugs and alcohol, crime, temptation with sex or whatever, it all existed when your parents were young. Young people today really do not pay enough attention to the things their parents have been telling them until it is too late. They wait until their defiant behavior becomes a lifestyle, and they shrug at consequences. Pretty soon their actions follow them into adult life, and there is a cost: no job, poor relationships, and the inability to take care of themselves.

As hard as it may seem to listen and obey, if you can teach yourself some discipline while you are young, life will be much easier in the long run. Throughout my life, I remember guys saying, "Oh well, I do not have to do the right thing yet because I have got time. One guy did not change his life until he was 28 and look at how good he turned out." Maybe it looked that way on the outside, but there were some changes going on inside that person. You just do not flip a switch and go from a con to a good guy. What you are saying is, "I'll outgrow it. I'll get mature soon enough."

There is no guarantee that you will survive that long. One stop by the police and one search of your vehicle is all it takes if they find something bad. Do you know how many people of color end up in prison for drug possession because they do not have a lawyer to get them off? Know now that a rebellious life has consequences. I learned this lesson the hard way from all the friends that I lost. They thought they were invincible. Not everyone will have the favor and good fortune that I have had. There are many men who lost their lives while disobeying their parents. There are many men who got hooked on drugs while disregarding the advice of their parents. There are no guarantees in this life other than you live and you will die one day. Everything else, only God knows.

I agree that technology has changed a lot, values in our world have changed, but principles never change. Your parents and authority figures are placed in your life to teach you the principles of life. Every individual has the freedom of choice, but not freedom of consequences when making bad decisions. Consequences are up to other people: a week in jail, a year in prison. Which is it? Somebody else decides, not you when you make some bad decisions. You want to stay out late at night and miss morning workouts? Fine, you can lose the starting spot on a football team, or be the guy who plays when the score is 48-0. Which would you prefer?

The principles, the rules of law, won't change. Why not soak up some knowledge and life lessons from your parents while you have a chance? One day, when things get tough, you will really need it. You'll think back and remember all the things they said to you: follow the rules, do your own work, treat others with respect. You may not have an active parent in your life, but there is most likely a teacher, preacher, coach, or someone else who advises you about life on a regular basis. There is somebody watching you. Do not turn them away.

See the blessing in having that person in your life and take advantage of the wisdom they share. When I look at the highly successful people in life, I notice that they had someone to listen to while growing up and it helped them. They always speak of a mentor or a piece of advice that someone told them that they held onto which made a huge difference in their life. It is a good thing to have a care-taker. Maybe it is your parents, someone in your church, or a shopkeeper.

I am still in pursuit of greatness and still have so much left of me to give. I have made multiple costly mistakes in my lifetime, and there are many things that I would do differently if I could, but I cannot. Life is not a series of "do overs", it is a series of "do betters." Since I cannot change the past, I realized that I could start living a new way right now in order to prepare for my future.

I want you to start now and have a head start. Have what I did not have: more discipline and more respect for the adults around me. I am writing this book so that you can learn from my mistakes. I had strong values instilled in me as a young boy, but I ignored them many nights when I was in the NFL. I went against what I was taught because, at the time, I thought that I knew better. I do not want you to just know better; I want you to do better. Be better than me. Be better than everyone that has come before you in your family. Most importantly, listen up when your parents speak because they know what they are talking about.

BREAK THE GENERATIONAL CURSE

A generational curse is essentially bad luck that is being passed down through your family. It could be not having a father in the home, not graduating from college, going to prison at a young age, joining a gang, or committing crimes. It is anything with a bad outcome that gets passed from generation to generation. That is something that has to stop. It is up to each individual to break any generational curse in your family.

Think of a generational curse like a chain of dominos. When one domino is tipped over, it falls and knocks over the rest of them. As humans, we can sometimes resemble a chain of dominos but our minds allow us to change that.

Although a bad pattern may have started in a family long before a child's birth, each person has a choice to repeat the cycle or not. A person can step out of that line of bad luck and choose a new path to start on with their life and family. I am a big believer in breaking the chain when necessary.

I heard someone say once that our life is a product of our decisions, not our conditions. What that means is that no matter where we live, how poor we are, or what is around us, we can make a decision to do something different and to be better. We hear stories on ESPN all the time of people who overcame adversity and decided to be better, so they changed their life. It can be done so do not make excuses. Instead, make some changes and make a decision that is worth sticking to.

I remember when my friend Ike met his dad for the first time. His dad was a former NFL player who played for the Bucs back in the day. Since I played for the Bucs, I tried countless times to locate his father so that they could meet. His entire life, Ike ran from the opportunity to meet his dad. Ike thought that his dad did not care because he was never there for him. Ike was 30 years old when he finally gave in and agreed to meet his dad. When they finally met, Ike broke down in tears. He said it was the best feeling in his life. Ike was so glad that he was finally able to let go of the hurt and the pain so that he could let his dad into his life. It healed Ike.

Ike is one of the toughest people I have ever met in my life. For Ike to open up, meet his dad, and then burst into tears, let me know that this healing process is absolutely necessary. Learn from that. Everything happens in its right time. Do not get caught up questioning everything. Let things flow naturally and embrace them as they come. Be open to meeting your parent one day if the opportunity comes; if it does not, know that the chance did not come for a reason.

A generational curse can extend beyond family and move into an entire age group. An age group could be living in a time period when drugs, sex and violence are at all-time highs. One can choose to fall victim to it or break free of it. That person can decide to give into it or be different and stand out in a distinct way. When I was in high school, I had a lot of friends who joined gangs and chose the thug lifestyle. Although I made many mistakes and did some things that I am not proud of, I decided to do better than to follow that path. Instead of giving my life to a gang, I chose to dedicate my life to the game I loved. There were times that I had to cut off some friends, separate myself from the crowd and be different. There were times when I wanted to do what the other boys were doing, but I chose not to. Sometimes, I had to get myself in the house early just to stay out of trouble. My life literally was saved because I decided not to go to a certain party or hangout with certain guys at night. I can look back over the years and see many instances when something different could have happened in my life had I made the wrong decision in a moment of pressure.

DECIDE TO BE THE ONE TO CHANGE

I t is rough trying to be a change agent if you did not have a father in the home, or if your parents were on drugs, or in prison. Suppose you had a brother or sister that joined a gang and went to prison. Maybe there has not been anyone in your family who has gone to college – a person can change that. be the one to make a difference; be the one that says, "I will be better than those around me and those who went before me. I will leave an imprint that will change the legacy of my family's name." Be the one to do that; it is just a choice that has to be made.

SEEK OUT WHAT YOU NEED

If you do not have a father in the home, then listen to your coach, your teacher, your pastor, your aunt or uncle or whoever is a respected figure in your life. Ask someone if you can talk to them; then tell them your secrets and get advice for your life. Look at their life, where they are, what they have been able to do and ask for some of their time. It may be one powerful statement they say to you that changes your life forever. They do not have to talk to you every day, every week or even every month. It may be one conversation that changes your life forever, so open up to someone and let them know your fears. Tell them about your family as well as your past and see if they can help you find a plan to break any generational curses within your family.

VOW TO DO IT DIFFERENTLY

If your father left your mother at an early age in your life or before you were born, then vow to yourself right now that you will always be there for your kids when they are born. If your parents did not go to college and you want to, make a vow to yourself that you will get into college and graduate. If your brother joined a gang when he was young, vow to yourself that you will never join a gang and you will live your life the right way. All of life is a choice.

EMBRACE YOUR LIFE

Know that if your parent was not there, then it is for a reason. Know that if the parent who neglected you was at least present in your life, then you could be worse off. Know that everything you need in your life is in you already. You were born with it and were built strong enough to make it without that parent. If they did not have it in them to be in your life, it is because they had some habits and flaws that you did not need to be around anyway. See it as a blessing, not a curse and do not blame or be mad at them for leaving. Understand it and embrace it. Let the hurt and pain go and embrace your strength.

If the day comes that you get to meet your parent who was not there for you, be mature enough to do so. Let the pain go and let him/her come in your life if they feel like they are ready. There may be a reason for them meeting you at thirty years old instead of at five years old. You do not know how you will react. Ike was angry all those years and then broke down in tears of joy.

BE GREAT

One of your goals may be to graduate from college. Well, that is what your academic counselor is for. You do not even need your parent's advice for that. The counselor at your school can tell you what classes you need to take and how to prepare for tests in high school. You can use that counselor to help you decide what schools you should look into and what grants and scholarships are available to you.

Resources are around to help you be different and break the generational curse. Do not feel trapped, as if you have to do what your parents or other family members did. Do not be afraid to be great. If anyone around you does not want you to do better for yourself, then they do not really care for you. An important key to success is to shoot for greatness in all that you do.

There will come a time that you have to let some people go in order for you to grow. Start today by moving towards a new life and breaking the cycle. Be better than your father; be better than your friends. Be better, different, bold, determined and dedicated.

DO NOT BE FOOLISH

A child is a parent's pride and joy, no matter how old that child gets. Keep in mind that how you act in public reflects how your parents have raised you. It is not always fair to parents because sometimes they teach us everything that we need to know, but we choose to disobey and do it our way. One thing I have realized is that the headaches you give your parents now will be the same that your own child will give you. It will be payback, in a sense. Sometimes, I wish I could go back and do some things differently, for my mother in particular.

My mother was a very proud woman. She always kept her head up and carried herself in a very classy way. I know she wanted more than anything to have a bunch of angels for kids; instead, she had me. I was a knucklehead at times. I was bold, daring and was not afraid to try new things. I was always getting into something. I did not do anything crazy enough to get me into trouble with the law, but I did enough to get caught up with my mom. My mother was a teacher, so it was her job to keep kids in line. Imagine how embarrassed she would be when her own son got into trouble. She was so strict that sometimes I felt like I could not do anything but let her down. I did not fully understand at the time why she was so strict, but it makes sense now that I am older and have kids of my own.

I remember an instance when my mom and dad went out of town to visit a sick family member. I hid my excitement as I waved goodbye to them, knowing I had the house to myself. As soon as they were out of sight, I started making phone calls. The house party of the year was about to go down. All my boys came over immediately. We invited all of the girls we knew and before we knew it, the cars started pulling in. All of my boys invited one girl to hang out with, but I had to be the show off, more like the fool, and invited every girl I liked, all of my ex-girlfriends and the girl I was dating at the time. Things did not go smoothly, but I was only 17 years old.

One of the girls crawled through my window, cornered me in my room with a butcher knife, and was about to gut me like a fish because I had so much going on at my house. My friend Ike was in the room with me. Lucky for me, he was there. I jumped behind Ike and used him as a shield as the young lady prodded the knife around Ike trying to land my flesh. Ike grabbed her hand and we all fell to the floor. I took the knife out of her hand and ran out of the room. Minutes later, the police showed up, and it was all downhill from there.

I thought that I could have a secret party without my parents knowing, but I was wrong. It was somewhat difficult to hide the multitude of cars parked up and down the street. My mom is a devoted Christian woman and does not do or allow parties. Imagine how angry my mom was. It completely embarrassed her to have the neighbors calling her and telling her that kids were running in and out of her house and the police were there. It hurts looking back on it, but that is why I am writing this – so you do not make the same dumb mistakes I made.

There were so many times I would get into trouble, and my mom would defend me even when she knew I was wrong. It drove her crazy and really affected our relationship in a negative way. I could not understand why she was so protective and by the book, and she could not understand why I was so free-spirited and disobedient. We definitely did not see eye to eye about a lot of things. When I went to college and then to the pros, I thought it would help mend some of the emotional wounds I dished out, but they are still there. When you hurt someone, it is easy to forgive, but never easy to forget. Now that I am older, I am ashamed that I never considered my mother's feelings. I was so selfish to hurt the woman who loved me first and would die for me. I betrayed her over and over again, but she never once stopped showing me her unconditional love. I cannot say sorry enough, Mom.

CONSIDER THOSE WHO LOVE YOU

Before you get ready to do something stupid next time, please think about how it will make your parents feel. Think about how other people might look at them and talk badly about them behind their backs because their child is unruly and disobedient. Think about how it will make their parenting skills look. Also, remember that what goes around comes around. If you make it hard on them, one day it is going to be hard on you, too. Mothers take their children's errant behavior much harder than fathers, and I am sure you have seen a few mothers cry over their child's behavior. I cannot fully explain why, other than embarrassment, hurt and shame. A foolish child brings shame to their parents, especially their mothers.

BE RESPONSIBLE

Strive to make your parents happy. Strive to repay them by being great in everything you do: school, work and life. Think about all that your parents have sacrificed so that you can have clothes, food, a place to live and a car to ride in. You do not want your mom to be the one who has to walk with her head down because her child is a delinquent. Love yourself and your parents enough to do what is right.

If you do not have a good relationship with your parents or if your parents are not the best in your eyes, do not let that be an excuse to be disobedient. Do not ruin your life just because they ruined theirs. Instead of carrying on that cycle, stand up and be different. Do something in a different way to get a better result. Let the fact that you may have a bad situation at home motivate you to be better than they did. If Dad or Mom chose to neglect their responsibilities of being a good parent, let that motivate you to grow up and be a great mother or father. A lot of people ruin their own lives while blaming their parents for what they did not do right. Do not be one of those people. Remember to make a decision to be in control of your own life and leave a positive legacy behind you.

NFL VETERAN LEADERSHIP:
SEPARATE YOURSELF FROM THE CROWD

Stand for Something or You Will Fall for Anything

I have seen so many guys, including myself, blow some great opportunities because we did not stay in the fight. It is common to set a goal achieve it, and then relax. It is human nature to arrive at that goal that we have always wanted only to do the opposite of what we did to get there.

What I have learned through all of my mistakes, all of my trials and tribulations, is that it is bigger than me. When I look back over the things I did in high school – becoming a father at 18, hanging out and partying while in the NFL, living recklessly at times in my life – I understand that it could have ruined me. I could have gone to jail in high school. I could have been arrested several times throughout my life. I could have lost my life in several situations if things had taken a different turn.

It is a celebration after we have arrived at the destination. And then, just like that, all that sizzled begins to fizzle. We can lose what we have earned in an instant. Success cannot just be attained, it must be maintained and, sometimes, maintaining it will be harder than attaining it.

After three years in the NFL and losing control, I began to change and turn around the negative balance. I had to get it right. I had to keep making deposits into my life, not deposits into my bank account. I had to get back to that mentality I had my rookie season and get myself out of the red. That is how I received the second deal with the Bucs, the one people did not think I deserved. I devoted myself to the game again. I was reinventing Michael Clayton, dusting off the old habits of resilience and hard work. I had one more year with the Bucs after I signed that deal. It did not completely work out, but I found my calling again. I was already on my path of change and I was not going to get detoured. The Bucs released me and I could have easily given up and thrown in the towel, but I had adopted a new mindset. I was getting back to my college ways. I was changing my life and doing it right.

The next option in mind was the UFL (United Football League). I did not want to go, but I decided to be obedient to what God was leading me to do. It was one of the most humbling experiences I have ever had. My high school football experience was better than this UFL experience, and as you know, you do not get paid in high school. In the UFL, we were playing at community centers and did not have locker rooms most of the time. It was rough. My pride took a beating. Michael Clayton, the best rookie receiver in the NFL in 2004, playing for peanuts.

I was becoming more humble by the day. If you let it, pride can get in the way of purpose because we all are accustomed to letting ourselves get in the way of fulfilling our true destiny. I believe that we are selfish beings whether we know it or not. If we do not recognize our ego, we can miss a life lesson very easily. Many times, ego is unrecognizable, which makes it difficult to fix.

I was still able to be a leader in the UFL. I had to stand for something, show strength, keep my faith and stay strong in what I believed. I believed that the UFL was a stepping-stone, so I acted accordingly. I could have easily started partying, smoking and taking this opportunity as a joke. Instead, I treated it as a job interview for the NFL. I took it as my probationary period on the job, stood strong and made it a good experience. In that moment, I realized that happiness is a choice and I could dictate my situation by what I choose to think and believe. I chose to think positively and believed that positive results would come of this experience. After spending a month in the UFL, I received the call from the NY Giants to come up. This is what I was working for; this is the call I had been waiting for.

ALLOW OBSTACLES TO PROPEL YOU

I almost killed my dreams of playing in the NFL again because of my fierce pride. Suppose that I had said "no" to the UFL? Do you think the Giants would have taken a chance on me? I had to find the strength deep inside myself to ignore what people would say about my decision. I had to believe that I could make it work even if it meant leaving my wife and kids behind for a month. I had to accept that life is not fair, nor is it easy. Many times it takes sacrifice along with hard work and dedication to get the results that we desire. Do not let the obstacles in life stunt your growth. Stand tall on obstacles and allow them to be stepping stones.

TAKE A STAND

If you do not stand for something, you will fall for anything, and your life can easily fall apart over anything. If you do not have any morals or values to help keep you intact, life can easily become difficult without anything to help you turn things around. You will exist, but you will not truly be living. In order to truly live and have an abundant life, you must stand for something.

BE A LEADER EVEN AMONG MEN YOU DO NOT KNOW

When I got to the NY Giants in 2010, I had to stay in the same mindset that had gotten me there. In fact, I had to step up my game a notch. The season had already started. It was Week 10. I could not get complacent and feel as if I had made it again. I had to make good on this contract. I knew that every day would be a battle, so I decided to continue leading. I am a natural born leader; I had to accept that role and stand with it. I could have just as easily slipped into trying to fit in and do things that I knew I should not do. Instead, I decided to stay as strong as I possibly could. I knew that I would fall sometimes, but I had to get back up and be transparent about my mistakes.

Now, my mistakes were not just for me, but they were also for the guys around me. I had to open up. It was my time to be the mentor. I spent a lot of time talking to the rookies and they knew that I was a first round draft pick who had an amazing rookie year and never got back to that year. They wanted to know, "What happened Mike?"

They wanted to know because they did not want to make the same mistakes that I did. I was able to speak to them in a very candid way and paint a picture for them very clearly. They could grasp this message and implement it into their lives. This teaching process was very important to me.

I realized that at this point in my career, I needed to play a different role on the team. It was my job to be a veteran leader in the locker room and not just be one of the guys. I knew that I would not see the field as much, so I had to lead in the locker room, from the sidelines and off the field. I had to walk right so that others could see my walk, see God in me and have a desire to know Him. I took pride in teaching and helping others understand what took me so long to learn. I gave the younger players messages that I did not get when I was in their shoes and felt it was my duty to give back. I would feel worthless if I did not give back from all the lessons I had learned up until that point.

We started having fellowship meetings on Wednesday nights. It started with four guys but quickly grew. I prayed for the team often, and they entrusted that to me. Here I was, basically a practice squad player, but I was able to affect some lives around me. They did not look down on me or treat me like crap. They treated me with respect and realized I had paid my dues. I was not a rookie trying to be a leader. I was a man who had made costly mistakes, had seen some ups and some downs, and had lessons to teach from my life experiences; the guys gave me a platform to share my story.

BELIEVE IN YOURSELF

You have to be willing to be a leader among men you do not even know. If you aren't careful, what others believe about you will become your belief about yourself so stay strong and believe in yourself.

BE AUTHENTIC

Do not be afraid to stand out in the crowd because you are different. Remember to remain humble in doing so. Do not be afraid to make mistakes because they are a part of life. Learn and grow through mistakes. Also, do not be afraid to be a devout Christian or man or woman of faith. If you are not afraid to be you, then others who are searching for themselves might follow you and you will be able to lead them to safe ground. Your actions might help others find themselves.

Leadership is an action. A person cannot just assume the title of "Leader". Going through a personal challenge can give the needed examples to teach others.

I can remember being in practices with the Giants. I was not on the practice squad, but I still took every practice rep against our number one defense to make them better. I made it my job to get the guys ready for what they were going to face on Sunday. This was my way of maximizing my full potential and getting involved anyway possible, so I chose to take it seriously. It was also the best way to prepare myself in case they needed me. I went as hard as I could and pushed the corner backs to be great. I made them work overtime with me. I broke them down and then built them back up. I told them what I was going to do to them, and then did it. After I did, I would help them understand how I was able to have success and point out their weakness. It was my time to teach several lessons all at once.

This was a good experience for me because it boosted my confidence and gave me a purpose on that team. I did it to the best of my ability and took pride in it. If I had to play special teams, then I would give it my all and I would not slack for any reason. The coaches would praise me in practice and the defense would watch me on film every day breaking them down. I had to find a way to lead and that leadership showed in my coaches' comments:

"Michael Clayton has great work ethic. A consummate professional." –*Coach Tom Coughlin,*

"Did you see the kickoff coverage when the 'off' returner came up and he just decked him and then the block on the long return and he just splattered him?" Coughlin said of Clayton. "If the young players could watch how that guy goes about his business, he is very intense and serious. Kind of fun to watch someone play like that because he really plays hard." *–2012 Giants vs Bears game, Coach Tom Coughlin,*

A tight end from my UFL team, Christian Hopkins, was signed to the Giants with me. I guess when they were looking at our UFL team, saw us both and decided to bring us in. He told me that I had touched his life and I was the reason he stayed strong and positive while in the UFL. Now, he had an opportunity again. That touched my heart because that is what I was working for. That represented and defined leadership in my eyes.

No matter where you go or who you are around, always be a leader. Stand for what you know is right and do not let it go. It does not matter what they say about you or how they treat you. If you stand your ground, eventually they will come around. Do not let anyone drag you down because if they drag you down, they definitely will not pick you back up.

FIND YOUR PURPOSE

There is a deeper meaning to life that numerous people do not understand right away. A person usually does not understand this until they have hit rock bottom. What is even worse is when someone hits rock bottom and they cannot get back up. Some people hit rock bottom and bounce back higher than they have ever been before and that defines their success.

As I look back, I see that God's grace has always been over my life. He has had his hand on my life in some way and has been my guiding force. I could be locked away in prison or dead and gone, but I am here. I have lost so many friends, but I am here. I have seen people fail and kill themselves, but I am here. I have seen so many people turn to drugs and lose everything they have, but I am here. As I look back, I know that it is not me alone, but it is all God who has protected me. That lets me know that there is something bigger in life. That lets me know that there is something I am supposed to do that is much bigger than me. This book is a step in that direction.

The 2011 season for the New York Giants was a divine year. God showed Himself to me and gave me a word to speak into each and every person on that championship team, including coaches. Not once did I ask God to help me make the team, for that might not have been His will. Instead I prayed for favor: favor in the eyes of my coaches; favor in the eyes of my teammates; and even favor in the eyes of the New York media. He granted me all of these things even in the face of adversity.

On opening day, I knew how I performed throughout training camp and in the preseason. I knew that I had made a good enough impression to make the team. I still got released. I remember the thought God placed in my head 15 minutes before the deadline, "I am not going to let you make this team my son that would be too easy. But when I bring you back, this is what I want you to say to the media." Right then, my phone began to ring; it was the New York Giants asking me to come into the office. I walked into Coach Tom Coughlin's office with a smile and told him how much of an honor it was to play for him and that he was the type of coach that got the best out of his players. I could tell on every coach's face that this was a tough decision to cut me, but they did. It was the business of football. They also told me to stay ready because as soon as someone went down, I could expect a call.

Thirty guys were cut that day, but Coach Coughlin told the world how difficult it was to cut guys like Michael Clayton. It was only a week or two that passed before I got that call to come back to the Giants.

I learned a lot from Coughlin – the importance of discipline, rules and attitude and structure. He would bring in quotes from war heroes and ask us to recite them. He based his whole coaching approach on having the right attitude. He preached punctuality and he set high expectations. He tried to instill the same culture with the Giants that Coach Saban tried to instill at LSU.

I had a week to week contract with the Giants. The role I assumed was to assist the younger players by acting as a mentor and showing a veteran's presence in the locker room. I really had to call on my skills as a veteran during the 2011 season after we had a bad game. Antrel Rolle, the safety from Miami, was so upset with the way we were playing. In front of all the players and coaches, he stood up in the meeting room and started screaming. He was screaming at specific people and using some pretty rough language. I could see Coach Coughlin's face getting red because he did not like that type of behavior. In my opinion, Coach Coughlin also wanted to respect Antrel's opinion.

After the meeting, I went to Coughlin's office. He was getting ready to do something to Antrel and punish him for all those things he said. I told Coach that 98 percent of the people in that meeting room did not agree with what Antrel said and that they were not going to pay attention to it. I tried to tell Coach Coughlin that some guys are from a different walk of life and they can sometimes go off like that. Coach understood what I was saying and told me that I had better talk to Antrel; that I should let him know that he could not act like that on the team. I told Antrel that he needed to apologize to the head coach and before I could say anything else, he said, "Mike, you're right. I should not have said what I said." He and the coach eventually got things straightened out.

I tried to have the same impact on Brandon Jacobs. He hails from my neck of the woods and the assistant coaches sometimes looked to me to help get him going. I tried to bring something different to the organization, in addition to special teams play. I had changed my lifestyle by the time I played for the Giants in 2011. I started going to the fellowship group on Wednesday nights with four players. Pretty soon we had 15 players and staff members. It was a chance for players to voice their opinion and talk about what was going on in their lives. It got to the point where on the sidelines at the Super Bowl someone came up to me and said, "Mike, we need one of those prayers. C'mon Big Bro." I started to pray and soon four or five people are touching me. When I said "Amen," Mario Manningham made that catch that helped us win.

The guys remembered how I told them all year that we were going to win the Super Bowl. I never prayed to make the team; I prayed for favor. One day I dropped the cross that I wear around my neck. As coach Mike Sullivan (current offensive coordinator for Tampa Bay Buccaneers) picked it up, Coach Coughlin wales by, sees me with my cross, digs into his pocket and pulls out his own cross. He winks at me and walks on.

The media found it odd that Coach Coughlin singled me out multiple times and I was not even a big contributor. It was not a routine thing for him to single out players, especially guys on the bottom of the roster. He was all about the team. But I had God's Favor and Favor can change a man. As I stood at my locker one day, every camera in the locker room stood in front of me waiting to hear what I had to say. I told them what God had done for me and how good He is. I was being obedient. If you Google my name and the New York Giants, this interview pops right up.

In week four, God told me that He was now ready to give me my heart's desire, which was to win a Super Bowl. Every day, I was on a mission to rally the word that "This was the year of the breakthrough." Every man that had joined our fellowship group enjoyed the journey and appreciated the weekly fellowship. What a joy it was for my teammates to walk up to me, hug me, and say, "Mike you said it," after we defeated the New England Patriots in the 2012 Super Bowl.

I want you to understand that everyone has a purpose. I want you to know that everything you are going through or have been through is for a reason. If you are a player on a roller-coaster journey like I was, embrace the lessons of every season and search deep to grab the meaning or reason. Respect the path your life has taken since it is a reflection of the decisions and choices you have made. Carry on in a way that will allow you to succeed because there is a reason for your existence.

You might ask, "Well, how do I find my purpose?" I have learned that the root of purpose is service. If I am not serving others, then perhaps I am not living a life of purpose. Some people only care about themselves. What can they get? Who can they become? Who do they have to take advantage of to get there? I used to be focused solely on myself, but then I got a wakeup call. Purpose is bigger than me. Whose life are you touching? Who are you encouraging or helping? How will you make the lives of others better? What type of charity will you start? What type of book will you write?

HELP OTHERS

Start living a life of purpose today by helping others. Volunteer at the local YMCA, Boys & Girls Club, or school. There are a number of websites with volunteer opportunities for all ages. Let your life serve as a vessel for others. If you have a gift or skills that others do not have, use it to teach. Go out of your way to make someone else's day. If you have lived through something and want to reach back and help those going through it now, then do it. If starting a movement is not an option, join someone else's until you can start your own. You know what they say:,"Have an attitude of gratitude."

What I have learned is that it is easy to believe that life is about how much money you can make and how many accolades you can accumulate. The hard thing to do is to realize that favor is far more valuable than any materialistic thing. Great things come to those who are good Samaritans. All that matters is what you have done to change the world around you in a positive way. Ask yourself, what have I committed to do in order to impact the lives around me? The answer to this question is what will matter the most. What did you create that will outlive you? What did you give back that will outlast you? Who will have a good story about you after you're gone? Also, your self-esteem is going to determine where you go in life so have confidence.

Some may want to be a pro athlete; that is all fine and dandy, but have a purpose for the success. After becoming a pro athlete, do not be satisfied with just being looked up to for your athletic ability. Instead, allow people to look up to you for the money you allocate to good causes in the community. Use the new found success as a platform to speak positively and effect change in the world. Do the right thing with your platform and your legacy will outlast you.

I started my foundation years ago, and now that foundation will be able to flourish and touch lives. I realize now that it is not about me; it is about the people. Every person that I meet now is someone that I want to impact in some way. When I die, I want people to remember me as a giver, a lover of people, and a servant leader. I want my purpose to be crystal clear. You should strive for the same thing.

REFLECTION

After you are done reading this book, sit down and grab a sheet of paper to write down what you want to do with your life. Write down how much money you want to make, but also put down how you want to use your time to help others. Identify a group of people that you want to help. Find those people and start helping now. At 30 years old, I can say I am truly blessed to have played in the NFL for eight years, have a beautiful wife, and three children. My personal goal was to play for two more years, but that was not my destiny. I can only control what I can control, which is to stay in shape and be ready for a call.

If for whatever reason, it does not work out that way, I know in my heart that my journey was never about chasing my rookie year, it was about the chase to discover the real me and my purpose in life. I will use the principles and lessons in this book to propel me toward success in life after football. I will also use this book to remind me of

God's saving grace and to encourage myself to continue to grow in my relationship with Him. Now, it is time for you to go out into the world and find your purpose.

Thank you for reading and God bless you.

28824704R00074

Made in the USA
Charleston, SC
23 April 2014